Effective Transition into Year One

Other titles by Alistair Bryce-Clegg:

Effective Transition into Year One

Alistair Bryce-Clegg

BLOOMSBURY

LONDON · OXFORD · NEW YORK · NEW DELHI · SYDNEY

Featherstone Education
An imprint of Bloomsbury Publishing Plc

50 Bedford Square
London
WC1B 3DP
UK

www.bloomsbury.com

FEATHERSTONE and the Feather logo are trademarks of Bloomsbury Publishing Plc

First published in Great Britain 2017

A catalogue record for this book is available from the British Library.

ISBN:
PB: 978-1-4729-3228-0
ePub: 978-1-4729-4951-6
ePDF: 978-1-4729-3227-3

2 4 6 8 10 9 7 5 3 1

Typeset by Newgen Knowledge Works (P) Ltd., Chennai, India
Printed and bound by CPI Group (UK) Ltd, Croydon, CR0 4YY

This book is produced using paper that is made from wood grown in managed,
sustainable forests. It is natural, renewable and recyclable. The logging and
manufacturing processes conform to the environmental regulations of the
country of origin.

To find out more about our authors and books visit www.bloomsbury.com. Here you
will find extracts, author interviews, details of forthcoming events and the option to
sign up for our newsletters.

Contents

Introduction

For some practitioners, the concept of play-based learning in Year One is a familiar one, but from my experience, that isn't the case for most. It certainly wasn't my experience as a Year One/Two mixed-age teacher. I was told in no uncertain terms that the time for play was well and truly over and it was time that the children actually did some 'work'! It is easy with your Early Years hat on to become very offended by this attitude. 'Work? How very dare you! What do you think we have been doing all year in Reception?' In many instances, I am not sure that we would want to hear the answer to that question. It will more often have the words 'messing' or 'faffing' or '*just* playing' in it.

I think we sometimes feel affronted because we have a different understanding of what a powerful learning tool play can be, because that is what we do every day and it is our 'bread and butter' when it comes to learning. If you have been trained as a teacher or a teaching assistant (TA) in the education climate of the last 20 years and have not been an Early Years specialist, then why would you see it any differently? Play has not been promoted as a learning tool. For lots of practitioners I work with in Key Stage One, play is something that you do in Reception and when you finish your work. It was a real turning point for me as a teacher when I realised that it was during play that children did their best work, and a lot more besides.

So, rather than seething quietly beneath our fleeces and tabards, venting our frustration with aggressive squeezing in the malleable materials area or with some angry tambourine shaking, we need to show how powerful and important play is and what amazing results a quality play environment can produce – especially in Year One and beyond. In reality, no matter how strong your own belief in a play-based curriculum is, it is *very* difficult to swim against the tide if you are getting lots of pressure from colleagues, senior management, Ofsted, etc. A headteacher once said to me: 'That is all well and good Alistair, but play theory won't get the SATs that I need'. And on it's own it won't, but that theory, applied by someone who knows what they are doing with support (especially from senior management) will get best outcomes for children (and they will probably exceed your SATs target).

I appreciate that in our fractured education system there is a *huge* amount of top–down pressure with unrealistic and inappropriate expectations for child development. Ideally the system needs to change, and that is something that we all need to push to make happen. But, that is not likely to happen anytime soon so in the meantime we have to teach creatively, making sure our practice is based on effective learning strategies and trying not to get too distracted by the other 'stuff'. What I am advocating is the 'bidet approach' where instead of top–down, all the thinking comes from the bottom up! That way we ensure that development and expectation are going in the right direction and are appropriate and realistic for the children in our care.

Just as most children do not have the same level of ability in every aspect of their learning, neither do they have the same level of development just because of their age – but there are many similarities. We know more than ever now about how the human brain and body develop. How children's ability to think and reason changes, how they refine their gross and fine motor dexterity... Yet none of this information appears to feed into the curriculum that we teach them in Key Stage One, or the way in which we teach it.

When a child enters Year One, they are only five (possibly six) weeks older than they were when they left Reception. In those weeks away from school their brain has been engaged in different ways of thinking and has been focused on all things that are not school. Little surprise then that lots of Year One children really struggle on their return. Not only are they going through a period of re-adjustment, they are often doing it in an unfamiliar space, with an unfamiliar person, with unfamiliar routines and a set of completely different learning expectations. When children first start in Reception you will often hear them ask, 'Is it mummy time yet?'. In Year One it is usually either, 'When is it time to play?' or 'Can we go outside?'. This can be frustrating as an adult, especially if you haven't got the provision or resources for play or going outside, but the children are telling you that they are not ready for, or benefitting from, this new 'formal' style of learning.

It is not that Year One teachers are not lovely, or that they are not working really hard. It is that the prescribed curriculum and methods of teaching are not meeting the needs of children at this age and stage of development. All is not lost however! Good transition into Year One can have a *massive* impact on children's wellbeing and therefore on their progress and attainment. Play-based learning can (and does) work in Year One (and beyond). But it is not as simple as getting the Lego™ out and letting them get on with it! As in EYFS, a successful learning environment looks like play and feels like play, but is under-pinned by knowledge, planning and rigour. (There! I used the 'R' word. It is always a good one to throw in when you are talking to someone who is nervous about play. It makes them feel a little bit more secure!)

As adults, we can find the transitions that we make in our life nerve-racking and unsettling. It could be starting a new job or moving to a new area. We often don't feel happy and settled until things become a bit more familiar. This sort of feeling is no different for children, in fact it is likely to be greatly magnified. As adults, we have a great deal of prior knowledge and experience of life to draw on, whereas children have significantly less. They don't know from experience that everything is likely to be all right, nor do they have strategies for dealing with the situation if it isn't.

That is why good transitions are crucial, both for children's emotional wellbeing, and their potential for attainment. The greatest inhibitor to attainment in schools is children's self-confidence and level of anxiety. When children feel comfortable and 'at home' in their environment they are far more likely to succeed. When they are subjected to significant change, it can take many children a long time to adjust to their new situation. During this period of adjustment their potential for maximum attainment is drastically reduced. To help to alleviate the anxiety that children might have, it is really useful when approaches to teaching and learning are harmonised at the point of transition. If children are moving between settings then this can be tricky, but if they are staying within a setting and moving to the next year group, it is a far simpler process.

As well as having some quality time to discuss transition with all of the adults who will be involved, it is really valuable to assess children's emotional welfare, wellbeing and involvement before and after transition. This will give you an accurate picture of how successful your transition has been. Tools like the Leuven Scales for wellbeing and involvement are a good resource for this. These are discussed in the next chapter (p.5).

One thing to keep at the forefront of your thinking is that children should enjoy the transition process – not just experience or endure it, but actually enjoy it. For this to happen, it needs to be planned well in advance. If it is practical, pre- transition visits should be regular throughout the year, not just in the last week of the summer term. The most important thing to remember about transition is that:

effective transition takes time, and is a process rather than an event.

1 A developmentally appropriate curriculum

Play-based transition

Over the years, when I have worked on transition projects, I have had lots of comments from Year One teachers saying how difficult they find transition and the concept of 'play'. All of them talked about the pressure that they feel (mostly from their senior management) to introduce a more formal learning style ASAP! I have also had a good few emails from Year One teachers who admit that they just 'don't get it'. They have never had EYFS training, never taught in the EYFS and therefore are not sure how they are supposed to magically become effective EYFS teachers. I have had a couple of comments along the lines of 'Get your head out of your own backside – the time for play is over; children need to start to get some work done. No wonder standards are falling in our schools.' And, 'It is all well and good to let the children play, but if I told my Year One children they could play all day, they would! Then when would the work get done?'

There have also been some (although significantly fewer) comments from Year One teachers who are already doing a play-based transition, or giving it a go – some with great success, others not so much and one who has already given up. When I tried to get to the bottom of what the people who were giving play-based transition a try were finding hard, they were all pretty much in agreement:

- lack of EYFS knowledge
- lack of equipment/resources
- lack of additional adults
- lack of support
- unrealistic expectations.

To be fair, if you are not quite sure what you are supposed to be doing and you haven't got any resources or support, it is going to be pretty difficult to put in place an effective transition model.

Through my project work with different schools and local authorities, I have also found out that people's definitions of 'transition' differ greatly. For some schools it is a couple of story swaps in the last week of term and that is it. For others it is a play-based approach to learning throughout the whole of Year One, and everything else in between.

I appreciate that even though it makes perfect sense to me and that there is significant evidence to prove it's appropriateness and effectiveness, the concept of children having play-based learning beyond Reception is one that is not accepted or promoted in the current educational climate in the UK. There are many very successful countries across the world whose children don't start their 'formal' education until they are seven years old. Indeed, three of Europe's most academically successful countries start school at seven years old. So a later start to more formal academic teaching does not mean slower progress.

High-level engagement is what gives you the potential for high-level attainment. The more engaged a child is, the more they absorb and facilitate their learning. We have to make sure that we are giving *all* children a developmentally appropriate approach to learning, which for the majority of children at five years old, 'formal' teaching isn't it. They are not physically, emotionally or academically ready to take on what is in essence a Victorian model of teaching and learning. Just because the children sit in silence and look at an interactive whiteboard rather than a blackboard doesn't make it a modern approach to learning.

Of course, children are not all the same; they will develop different skills at different times. I find practitioners will often tell me that they have a group of children that are 'ready for formal'. Likewise, I work with some schools that have a Year One class and a split Year One/Reception class where the 'less able' Year One children are in the split class because they 'need the play'. The truth is, they all need play – even the most able. It is through quality play experiences that children will be engaged and challenged, and that is how you facilitate truly effective learning.

In a BBC news article about the subject of a delayed start to school, Nichola Rutherford discusses research findings by Emeritus Professor of Education, Donald Christie:

'Where the start of formal education is delayed until children are seven, Prof Christie says that those who would have been capable at four are not affected and the children who would have struggled have had time to mature.' (Rutherford, 2016)

Even if we agree that children would benefit from starting school at seven years old, it is unlikely to happen tomorrow or in the near future. So, why am I telling you this? Well, as Year One teachers it might help to explain some of the issues that you struggle with – especially around engagement, attention span and behaviour – and help to shape an approach to teaching and learning that is more developmentally appropriate. Also to reassure you that quality play is an effective learning tool for the most able, not something they only get to do when they have finished their work, or on a Friday afternoon.

An effective learning environment

Happy children make successful learners and happy adults make successful teachers! So we need to make sure that we are all as happy and relaxed as we can be in school. For children entering Year One, the more the environment, resources and routines are as they were in Reception, the easier the transition will be. If the children have had several opportunities to visit their new Year One space and spend time with their (new) adults, the high level of familiarity will significantly reduce their conscious and subconscious anxiety. For adults setting up a Year One environment, the more you understand about EYFS practice, the more relaxed you will be. Add into this mix some appropriate resources, outdoor access and another fully trained adult, and you will probably be able to at least halve your alcohol consumption in the first few weeks of term.

High levels of wellbeing for all of us are crucial if you want to ensure success. It doesn't matter how fabulous you are or how amazing your classroom is, if a child (or adult) is feeling out of their comfort zone, they will not be firing on all learning cylinders! Imagine you have got a new job in a brilliant school with really lovely people, but you have been to the school only once before you applied and once on your interview. Today is your first day, how do you feel? Probably not at your most spectacular, and you are an adult not a five-year-old! One highly effective tool to help practitioners to create an effective learning environment and then monitor its effectiveness is the Leuven scales of wellbeing and involvement.

The Leuven scales of wellbeing and involvement

The Leuven scales were developed by the Research Centre for Experiential Education at Leuven University, under the supervision of Professor Ferre Laevers in 1994, and have become a well-recognised and welcome addition to effective assessment. 'Wellbeing' refers to children's self-esteem, self-confidence and resilience, described by the Leuven

Institute as when children behave 'like fish in water'! 'Involvement' refers to their levels of engagement, interest and the depth of their learning. Each scale has five levels.

Wellbeing scale

Level 1 – Extremely low
Children clearly show signals of discomfort. They may:

- whine, sob, cry, scream
- look dejected, sad or frightened or panic
- be angry or furious
- be aggressive, kick with feet, wriggle, throw objects, hurt others
- suck their thumb or rub their eyes
- not respond to the environment, avoid contact, withdraw
- hurt themselves, bang their head, throw themselves on the floor.

Level 2 – Low
The posture, facial expression and actions indicate that children do not feel at ease. However, the signals are less explicit than under level 1, or the sense of discomfort is not expressed all of the time.

Level 3 – Moderate
Children have a neutral posture. Facial expression and posture show little or no emotion. There are no signals indicating sadness or pleasure, comfort or discomfort.

Level 4 – High
Children show obvious signs of satisfaction (as listed under level 5). However, these signals are not constantly present with the same intensity.

Level 5 – Extremely high
During the observation episode, children show enjoyment and appear to feel great. These children:

- look happy and cheerful, smile, beam, cry out of fun
- are spontaneous, expressive and really themselves
- talk to themselves, play with sounds, hum, sing
- are relaxed – do not show any signs of stress or tension
- are open and accessible to the environment
- are lively, full of energy and radiate

- express self-confidence and self-assurance.

Involvement scale

Level 1 – Extremely low
Children hardly show any activity:

- no concentration – staring, daydreaming
- an absent, passive attitude
- no goal-oriented activity, aimless actions, not producing anything
- no signs of exploration and interest
- not taking anything in, no mental activity.

Level 2 – Low
Children show some degree of activity but this is often interrupted:

- limited concentration – look away during the activity, fiddle, dream
- are easily distracted
- any action leads only to limited results.

Level 3 – Moderate
Children are busy the whole time, but without real concentration:

- carrying out only routine actions, attention is superficial
- not absorbed in the activity, activities are short-lived
- have limited motivation, no real dedication, do not feel challenged
- do not gain deep-level experiences
- do not use their capabilities to full extent
- the activity does not address the child's imagination.

Level 4 – High
There are clear signs of involvement, but these are not always present to their fullest extent:

- children are engaged in the activity without interruption
- most of the time there is real concentration, but during some brief moments the attention is more superficial
- they feel challenged, there is a certain degree of motivation
- their capabilities and their imagination are to a certain extent addressed in the activity.

Level 5 – Extremely high

During the episode of observation, children are continuously engaged in the activity and completely absorbed in it:

- they are absolutely focused and concentrate without interruption
- they are highly motivated, persevere
- even strong stimuli cannot distract them
- they are alert, show attention to detail and precision
- their mental activity and experience are intense
- they constantly address all their capabilities – imagination and mental capacity are in top gear
- they obviously enjoy being engrossed in the activity.

In many of the transition projects I have done, we have used the Leuven scales at the end of the third term of Reception and then again (with the same children) on entry to Year One. Lots of members of staff have been amazed by the significant drop in many children's wellbeing and involvement on entry to Year One compared with what it had been in Reception. If their wellbeing and involvement are low, then the potential for achievement and progress is also low.

The perils of striving for a good level of development (GLD)

National statistical data tells us that 66.3% of children achieved a good level of development (GLD) at the end of Reception 2015 (DfE, 2015). So that means that 33.7% of children didn't (amazing maths skills I know!).

If you think back to the summer term, you may have felt the very tangible pressure that your Reception team were under to make sure that the maximum number of children made GLD. Often what happens is that as a result of year-on-year target setting, and performance management pressure, practitioners will identify where the 'gaps' are that are prohibiting certain children from reaching the desired GLD target. Once the gaps are identified, the teaching and learning is planned in such a way that lots of opportunities are taken to fill the gaps using more specific activities such as extra sessions of phonics, extra reading at lunchtime, etc.

In some Reception settings, under the guise of 'school readiness', in term 3 children are given more formal, structured, adult-led teaching and less 'continuous provision' (see Chapter 3, p.27). The sand and water may disappear to make room for extra tables. (If this style of teaching is not developmentally appropriate in Year One, then there is little hope if it is introduced in Reception). By the end of this intense period of 'coaching', children will often be able to produce evidence to show that they have filled the gaps and are now at a GLD. This evidence is often moderated by Year One staff, senior management and sometimes local authority moderation teams. The evidence is robust – the children can do it – at the time. But, because a lot of this information has been learned at speed in a short space of time, it doesn't stick. We give those children five or six weeks off on holiday and then they return to a Year One environment that is nothing like their Reception experience – it is little wonder that the learner a Year One teacher has sitting in front of them appears very different from the children who achieved the GLD in the summer. It is just like when we revise/cram for a test. How much of that information becomes part of our hard-wired knowledge base and how much seems to leak out of our brain while we are asleep?

Of those 66.3% of children who achieved a GLD, I would hazard a guess that they were not all still secure with their learning on entry to Year One. Those children aside, you potentially have a third of your class who have not yet reached a good level of development with a play-based approach to learning. They are *very* unlikely to flourish with a more formal approach on entry to Year One. I firmly believe that you will reap the biggest rewards if you pitch the start of your year in Year One at the appropriate level for all children in your class by taking into account an effective transition, the link between wellbeing and achievement and what a powerful learning tool play can be. Pushing children too soon into a developmentally-inappropriate learning environment, in the hope that they will learn more at a faster pace, will actually make your job and their learning significantly harder. This will make you fed up and stressed and make them stressed and fed up!

It is okay – in fact more than okay – to provide a quality play environment for children on entry to Year One. It is also okay to stand back and observe your children, their interactions, interests and learning preferences. You often learn so much more by watching than you do trying to get through your 'groups'. It is perfectly appropriate to evidence what you are seeing in the same way that it is done in Reception with photographs, observations, discussion, creations and practitioner judgment. Although it is important that we are able to show children's achievement progress, this doesn't have to be written in a book. What children are able to record at this age is a tiny aspect of what they know and can do. It is wrong to make judgments about their ability based only on what they record in a book. In the words of Einstein:

> 'Everyone is a genius. But if you judge a fish by its ability to climb a tree, it will live its whole life believing that it is stupid.'

When it comes to a play-based approach in Year One, I know that lots of you will be thinking that you haven't got the resources or the space or the staff. Although effective play-based transition requires all of those things, fundamentally it is an ethos. It is important to be clear about what effective transition should look like and then work towards that goal.

2 Building on what they know

Use assessment to create an environment for learning

In order to create the ideal transition environment for the start of Year One, you need to map your space and create your environment plan. Your EYFS team will actually have started this for you. Their last summative assessment in the summer term will provide you with all of the information that you need to create your cunning plan. They will have assessed all of their children against the areas of learning (17 in all). They will have data on which children are performing below, in line with and above their age-related expectations.

With this information, I would create a Gap and Strength Analysis (GSA) – hopefully your EYFS team are doing this every time they do a summative assessment anyway, so they may have done the job for you. As I do for the Early Years teams that I work with, I would suggest that you create a GSA following every summative assessment that you carry out. This will be your blueprint for mapping your space.

Please note that a GSA is very different to making a gap analysis for an individual child as a 'hothouse' for GLD, referred to in Chapter 1 (p.10). A GSA is cohort wide and supports provision as well as teaching focus.

Gap and Strength Analysis (GSA)

A Gap and Strength Analysis is exactly what it sounds like. It identifies where your biggest learning gaps are and also where your children have areas of strength. You will use the information to help you to plug the gaps and create challenge where there are areas of strength.

If your EYFS team is already completing this sort of assessment and analysis, your first GSA will have been done for you. If you are unfamiliar with the Early Years 'jargon', then ask your team. Some settings will be using a commercially bought assessment tool while others will create their own. Expectations for children in EYFS can be found in *Early Years Outcomes*, which is a revision of *Development Matters in the Early Years Foundation Stage*. Both are useful to have a look at.

Once you have completed your assessment, you need to identify the children who are performing *below* the age-related expectation in each of the prime and specific areas of learning. When I complete a GSA with a setting, I always encourage them to include any children who have just tipped into the expected age band, as they are emergent learners and still at risk of not reaching their expected levels of development. Using the same assessment, you are also going to identify the children who are performing *above* the expected age-related score in each of the prime and specific areas of learning. These children are demonstrating a high level of capability and you need to ensure that you have catered for their needs with challenging and open-ended resources.

Some settings will only ever identify areas for development in their GSA because their cohort come in so much below the expected point of entry age-related statements. Some, on the other hand, will have a significant number of children who start Year One above the expected point of entry. As always, you work with what you have got! The important thing is that you show that you are using your assessment to inform your planning – from the space that you create, right down to your direct teaching.

Make a graph

Once you have gathered all of this lovely data, the best thing to do with it is to make a graph. Why a graph? Well, because everybody loves a graph and you want your data to be presented in the most visual and user-friendly way possible.

Here is an example of a GSA for a Reception class in the summer term as the children are preparing for their transition into Year One. After assessing each child's development against their age-related statements in the prime and specific areas, the following analysis was produced. It is important to note here that your GSA is entirely focused on your current cohort. No two years are likely to be the same.

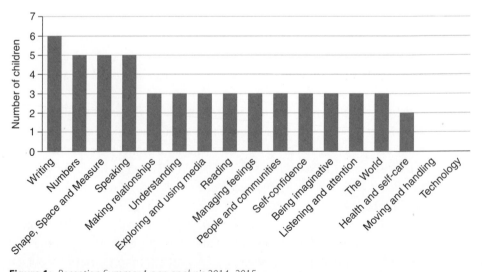

Figure 1: *Reception Summer 1 gap analysis 2014–2015.*

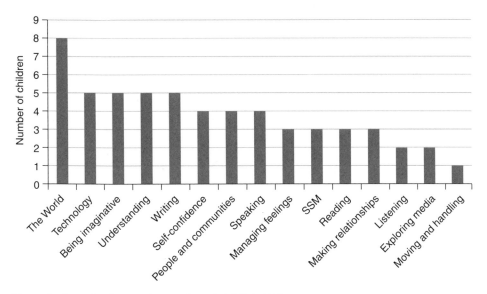

Figure 2: *Reception Summer 2 strength analysis 2014–2015.*

Your next step is to interpret your data and then apply it to your space. This is the interesting and sometimes tricky bit! If nothing else, your GSA should enable you to talk about the needs you have identified and how you are going to tackle them. If we take the GSA in figures 1 and 2 as an example, I would want to agree with my team on what constituted a significant 'gap' that might need some significant 'tackling' and what was more of a day-to-day need that could be tackled on an individual level. It would be up to your team or senior management to make a judgement call on what you or they felt would constitute a 'significant gap' and that is were you would start.

In the example above, the chart clearly identified the areas of need, and discussion between staff was able to shed light on why some areas were higher than others.

- Following the GSA, 'Writing' was a huge focus by all teaching staff. Extra writing opportunities at dinner times were planned for. Writing is an area that continually needs developing and staff are working together to further develop this area through linked provision (see Chapter 5, p.55), continuous provision (see Chapter 3, <p.27>) and focused writing sessions linked to the children's needs and interests. Out of the six children identified, three are new arrivals and do not speak English, and the other three are on the SEN register. Specific one-to-one sessions are planned to take place during summer term two.

- 'Number' and 'Shape, Space and Measure' are areas that staff were aware of as needing to be continually developed. All children are currently taking part in weekly challenges and linked provision activities twice a week. Daily meetings between staff regarding how continuous provision can help develop the areas of learning identified in the GSA will continue during summer term two. Three out of the five children identified are

Building on what they know

new arrivals and do not speak English. One child is on the SEN register and the other child is being closely monitored.

- It was discussed that the children identified as working below in 'Speaking' development were all children with English as an additional language or non-English speakers. It was decided that a member of staff would work with these children on a daily basis as an intervention. The importance of this prime area for all the children was talked about and ways in which this area could be developed for all children through activities and resources were considered. Ideas regarding specific focus tables and a 'talk sofa' were discussed and linked to the children's interests and themes.

Environment plan

Once you have produced your data, you now need to think about how that data is going to impact on the environment itself. You know the areas of learning that you are now going to promote. It is important that you record this process before moving onto the next step of your plan. Make an environment plan. In your environment plan, you will record the areas of learning that you are focusing on. Then you are going to list all of the areas of provision that you think have the most potential to help you to fill that gap.

Focused areas of learning	Areas of provision

Figure 3: *Environment plan.*

The Characteristics of Effective Learning are a useful starting point when considering your areas of provision (see below). Chapters 3 and 4 will also help you consider different areas of provision and formulate your environment plan (p.27–54).

Characteristics of Effective Learning in the learning environment

The Characteristics of Effective Learning should underpin everything that we do in our EYFS environments, and here I will look at how they can be applied to a Year One environment, where their impact is just as significant to all children's learning. They are fundamentally based in the science of how children learn and therefore should guide and support how we create learning spaces and how we teach. Although I am sure that you are all very familiar with them, it is always worth reminding ourselves of their importance before we go on.

Like sacred amulets, there are three of them. Each powerful in their own right, but together their combined power is immense! The characteristics of effective learning are:

- playing and exploring
- active learning
- creating and thinking critically

Playing and exploring

As discussed in Chapter 1 (p.5), the term 'play' is open to lots of interpretation and often has quite negative connotations, especially when you get into Year One and beyond. In truth, play is a very powerful teaching tool that – when you get it right – can have massive impact on children's wellbeing, engagement and therefore attainment.

A playful environment is one that has been structured around the needs of children and also provides them with support, challenge, ambiguity and interest. If an environment is too prescriptive, then you remove a great deal of it's potential to engage children in the learning process. When you think about 'exploring', climbing mountains or trekking through the jungle might come to mind, but when we apply the term to a learning space it just means that we give children's thinking somewhere to go. If we want our children to be creative higher-order thinkers, then we have to give them the opportunity to use the skills and knowledge that they have acquired. If they are motivated and interested by the environment that we create for them, they will want to explore it further. If we can then enhance that space further still, with resources and activities linked to that interest which will inspire creativity and thinking, then we have got ourselves a space that is truly set up for play and exploration.

Does your environment encourage children to play and explore?

- Do individual children show a preference for a particular area?
- Are the children being challenged by that area or just rehearsing familiar skills?
- Are children's interests reflected in your environment or is it solely linked to your topic or theme?

Is your space linked to children's preferences?

- Do your children have the opportunity to draw on their own experiences from home?
- Have you enhanced your learning space with interest-linked resources?

- Are the children confident in finding tools, materials and resources they need for a particular project?

Does your space encourage independence?

- Have you created activities or experiences that enable children to persist, revisit, and retry?
- Can children self-access their own resources or only use the ones that have been put out for them?
- Have you created a space that encourages children to rely on adult support or do they show initiative and independence?
- Are children keen to try new ideas or do they tend to stick with the familiar?
- Do you provide time for children to be reflective? Can they identify things that haven't worked and give possible reasons why?

Active learning

We are not just thinking body active here, we are also thinking brain active. There can be a culture in education of 'spoon-feeding' our children. We know what it is we want them to learn about so we teach that, then we give them activities or exercises directly related to thing we wanted them to learn. They complete those activities and we let them know if they are right or wrong. If a child is an active learner, they will undoubtedly need some of the input and scaffolding that we offer them to impart new information, but what they also need are lots of opportunities to apply that knowledge in different situations.

In an active learning environment, we need to think about how we help children to acquire skills, not just take part in activities. We want their knowledge to be transferable and not just fixed into their brain as an event or an experience.

How can you create an active learning space in Year One?

- Have you given the children the opportunity to stay focused on a self-initiated activity for a long period of time or are they heavily timetabled?
- Is there time for the children to show high levels of concentration without distraction?
- Are they 'intrinsically motivated' – achieving things for themselves as opposed to just looking for praise?
- Have you linked your learning objectives to children's interests so they demonstrate concentration through silent focused work or by talking out loud?
- Do you see evidence that the children enjoy what they are doing rather than just complying with instruction?

An environment for effective active learning

An 'environment for effective active learning' sounds like such an obvious statement. What other sort of environment would we create for our children to learn in? It is when we begin to unpick what 'effective learning' might look like that we begin to see the complexities of the task in hand. Whatever the size and shape of your space, your environment has the potential to have a significant impact on children's levels of engagement. The key is to make sure that children feel ownership of the space and that how you have arranged the resources and the content of your display are for the children and not you.

When thinking about planning for your environment, it's important to remember that it encompasses both indoors and out. Outdoor provision is such a crucial part of the EYFS curriculum that it receives equal weighting in terms of planning and resourcing as indoors. Unfortunately, in Year One it is often either not available or it is the poor relation, and the lack of provision results in a huge number of missed opportunities, especially for those children who it can be harder to engage indoors.

A good play-based environment will always have a healthy amount of child-generated mess on any given day: the odd handprint on the wall, splash of paint on the lino and unidentifiable stain on the carpet! Notice that I said 'child-generated' mess. There is a significant difference between the mess that children make when they are engaged in a learning process and the sort of mess that adults leave lying around. We are creating and maintaining a learning environment for children. Any adult 'stuff' should be filed or piled in a cupboard or drawer and not left on display for all to see.

Early Years practitioners are often very used to active mess – but it can be a bit of a shock to the system if you haven't had it before in Year One. Remember, our focus should be on teaching children 'process', and you can't teach process without a bit of experimentation, trial, error and mess!

Creating and thinking critically

This characteristic of learning is all about thinking. We need to give our children lots of opportunities to think, puzzle and work things out on their own and with others. At times in their development they will need a lot of scaffolding for their thinking, but at others they will need the opportunity to think for themselves – and that can be a little bit scary!

We are aware that babies and young children are thinkers who make sense of their experiences through perceiving patterns and developing concepts. As children engage in all the different activities that take place in the Early Years setting, they actively think about the meaning of what they are doing. Over time they will begin to become more aware of their own thinking – this is known as metacognition.

The more you focus on recognising different children's approaches to learning, the more skilled you will become at 'interpreting' what you see and then feeding that knowledge back into your environment and planning. The truth is that you can only recognise what you already know. The more you improve your own knowledge about how children learn, then the more you will see when you watch them in play and learning.

How can we encourage children to come up with their own thinking and ideas about their learning?

- Are there opportunities for independent learning in our classroom space?
- Do children have opportunities to retain their independence, not asking for help even if it takes them longer to complete the task?
- Do you build in time during your day for children to talk about how their actions or thoughts link to a previous event or experience?
- Do children draw upon knowledge or experience that is not immediately related to this activity?
- Can they use trial and error approaches and talk about why some things do and some things don't work? This will also require time and space within your day or week.
- Do they choose different ways of approaching activities and adapting that approach if it doesn't work?

An environment for thinking

I appreciate that thinking is something that we all do all of the time. But like everything else in life, there are levels of thinking. Often we think about the mundane and necessary, the day-to-day 'stuff' that keeps life running smoothly. But it is when we have opportunities to take our thinking beyond the mundane that we open up the possibilities for real creativity and innovation. As a Year One practitioner you have the capacity to create environments, plan experiences and model strategies that give your children the tools and the opportunities to become truly great thinkers.

What makes a good thinking environment?

A good thinking environment is one where children can learn new thinking skills, but then be given the opportunity to apply them. There are three primary strands to an effective thinking environment:

- **The characteristics of children's learning and thinking** – this is not about what your children have learned but how they learn, their particular motivations, personal preferences and learning styles.

- **The role of the adult** – it is the adults that will be responsible for creating the environment that supports children's learning styles and then facilitating opportunities for effective and productive thinking.

- **The physical environment** – an environment needs to be created that will support children in clarifying what they already know while also giving them opportunities to extend their thinking.

Before you can enhance children's thinking spaces, you need to first recognise how they think and learn.

Observing

Observing is very normal practice in the Early Years, but in Year One it can sometimes be perceived as a bit of a waste of time. Why stand and watch when you could be teaching?

It is really important, as a Year One teacher, to take time to plan yourself out of activities so that you can observe the children, track their interests, their preferred areas of play and how they are thinking. Are children already problem-solvers? Do they stick at a task until it is done? Do they give up when things become difficult? Do they ask for help before trying for themselves? During this period of observation, if you feel it is appropriate, engage with children in their play and exploration to further investigate their creative and shared thinking processes.

Developing

Once you have got a good idea about the sorts of strategies your children are using in their independent play and social interactions, we can use modelling, scaffolding and questioning strategies to extend children's thinking. If we use our knowledge of children's interests to support the context of the scenarios we create, then the children are far more likely to engage and learn.

Enhancing

When children are aware of different strategies for thinking, it is up to the adults to provide open-ended tasks that encourage children to think for themselves. Adults can ask children to 'think differently' or 'think creatively' – this will help children to focus their thinking.

Reflecting

Regular reflection is crucial in all aspects of practice. Adults need to reflect on whether and how the strategies that they are putting into place are having an impact on children. They also need to encourage the children to reflect on what they have learned about different ways of thinking.

Ambiguity

When it comes to developing creative and sustained thinkers, a good dollop of ambiguity can hold the key. Although in some aspects of their development children need very clear guidance and firm structure, it is always good to have an element of your practice and provision that will enable children to draw on their own experiences to form a conclusion. This can come in the form of your responses when they ask you for guidance and support. Rather than saying, 'Do it this way', or 'Try that', you can answer their question with another question to get them thinking, for example: 'What do you think would happen if…', 'I am not sure, how could we find out?'. Sometimes they will have an idea and sometimes they won't. This is where your modelling comes in.

Ambiguity isn't just limited to questions; open-ended resources and activities that rely on children's creativity and imagination will promote higher-order thinking skills. In your small world area, a cow will always be a cow, but a wooden block can be anything depending on whose hand it is in. Ambiguous, open-ended resources should be a must in every area of provision.

As well as being a great aid to learning, ambiguity can also be a bit daunting for some children, especially if they are not used to thinking for themselves. An effective questioning environment is not just about how effectively the team can model thinking skills, or how many open-ended resources you have got.

For these strategies to work, the children have to:

- Feel confident enough to 'have a go' and be able to express what they are feeling and what they are thinking.
- Have the language to be able to explain their thinking in a way that someone else can understand, talk about what they have done and begin to plan what they might do next.
- Show a level of imagination and creativity in their talk and play – a good imagination is a very useful tool to a creative thinker.
- Demonstrate motivation and an eagerness to learn, even if it is only in the subjects that really interest them. If they have not got an eagerness to learn, then they are unlikely to stick with a problem until its resolution.

Some of these skills children will learn through their individual experiences within the environment, but their progress will be significantly enhanced by the effective role of the adult within a quality learning environment.

As adult 'facilitators of thinking', we need to actively seek out opportunities to challenge and extend children in their thinking. Create activities and areas of provision that have been deliberately set up to encourage creative thinking while ensuring that children feel valued and supported, even when they feel that things are going wrong. Marion Dowling has produced a set of prompts for the role of the adult in promoting the idea of 'sustained shared thinking'. They show that adults can use both verbal and non-verbal communication to develop positive interactions assisting in the development of children's thinking skills. She says that adults need to:

- tune in
- show genuine interest
- respect children's own decisions and choices
- invite children to elaborate
- recap
- offer personal experience
- clarify ideas
- remind
- use specific praise
- offer an alternative viewpoint
- speculate
- reciprocate
- ask open questions
- use model thinking.

So, the role of the adult is pivotal in ensuring successful outcomes, but there are only ever a certain number of adults in one setting and they cannot be everywhere all of the time.

Another useful strategy for success is creating opportunities for children to work together to learn from and model for each other. Talking to someone else is a great way of getting ideas straight in your own head and getting someone else's opinion on whether your ideas will work or not.

Usually, this type of peer work needs support and guidance from an adult, especially when it comes to the type of questioning and language that the children might use in discussion with each other.

Through really effective collaborative discussion with their peers, children can learn to:

- Ask questions that are related to the discussion (not always easy).
- Develop their own ideas rather than just sticking resolutely to the first point they made.
- Explain 'why' they think what they think.
- Learn not only to be quiet when other people are speaking, but actually listen to what they are saying and (sometimes) comment on it.
- Change their idea based on what they find out (and not just because their friend had a different idea!).

Although set 'thinking times' (when children are given scenarios to think about and problems to solve) can be useful, you will have greater success if you aim to create a 'thinking environment' where key thinking skills are promoted and enhanced at all times.

What makes an effective 'thinking and doing' space?

We are often very timetabled in our approach to the Year One day. Direct teaching sessions are punctuated with assembly, playtime, lunch and PE. Where Year One children would really benefit – especially, but not exclusively, during transition – is to have a space that:

- promotes their independent thinking
- gives them time to think, and think again.

In good EYFS practice, and as I argue in this book, also in good Year One practice, the opportunity for effective thinking presents itself regularly during periods of continuous provision (discussed in the next chapter, p.27), where the children are not confined to learning with a particular activity or resource but are given access to a variety of resources and the time to explore them.

The more open-ended and ambiguous the resources you give children are, the more that you will prompt them into thinking and employing creative strategies for problem solving. Open-ended resources have a high level of ambiguity, which means that different children will use them in different ways, but they will still be exploring the same concepts. If you give your children a farm set to play with, they are likely to play their version of 'farm' because that is what the resources are inviting them to do. If, on the other hand, you create less prescriptive, more open-ended opportunities for play, then the possibilities for investigation and re-investigation are endless. A good thinking environment should be stimulating to children with a wide selection of materials that encourage exploration and investigation.

As an adult working with Year One children in continuous provision, you might have an idea about the learning that you want to enhance their play with. You might even have some next step objectives that you would like to deliver while you are working with them. But, it is important that any adult going into a situation where a child is showing self-direction and motivation learns to look at the play, make a judgement and then look again. What you don't want is an adult with a tick list 'picking' off children one by one to get their objective in regardless of what the child is doing. We want adults who will look, observe, enhance, scaffold, manage, reset and teach. Sometimes your objective will be really appropriate to fit in with or enhance the play. But often, what they children are doing will be nothing to do with your objectives but will be very valid in it's own right. That play needs to be valued and supported and not shut down.

To sum up, we would like to enable our children to be good creative thinkers who work in an environment that has lots of open-ended opportunities to enable creativity, that makes links to previous learning and provides challenges and moments of reflection as well as a healthy dose of ambiguity!

3 Continuous provision

You may have heard your Early Years team talk about 'continuous provision'. This is the bit of the day where the children are not having a direct adult input and are 'free' in the provision that has been created. As a Year One teacher who is used to working a system of 'carpet to table and then back to carpet', this will be a little bit scary – but stick with it, because when done well it is an amazing way to teach and learn.

When I was in Year One, my play-based provision amounted to the number of free corners that I had available (usually four). In these four corners I would put some play opportunities based on what was available. Not sand – too messy! Not water – are you kidding? Not dough – think of the carpet... I also needed to be sure that I was linking all play to visible academic outcomes – ideally literacy and numeracy. So, I would have a shop (counting, money and writing), a construction area (counting and measuring), a writing table (for even more writing) and often a 'nature' area because it gave me somewhere to put all of the conkers that the children brought in!

The problem with this approach is that it is not providing quality play experiences, it is not building on children's learning and it is probably encouraging the children to stagnate in their play and focus on a level of skill they have already surpassed. If you can give up your whole classroom space to continuous provision, then you will have a lot more room to play with. But if (like most Year One classrooms) you have limited space due to storage/furniture and you are having to work with four corners, then your GSA will indicate which areas of learning should take priority. That doesn't mean that you only have to offer continuous provision in your four corners; you can use your carpet and tabletops. Realistically, working in four corners means that you can't offer the range of choice and experience that you might ideally want to, but it is better than offering no choice at all.

One thing that will really help you and your team, especially with your planning for continuous provision, is to think about the Early Years settings that your children will be coming from, and think about *why* they have the particular areas of provision. What skills can children learn when they are playing and learning in them? It is worth considering at this point (and we will come back to this), that continuous provision is not something you go on to when you have finished your work. It isn't a holding activity or a 'reward'. It is a space for children to learn in the absence of an adult. Therefore it must be planned and considered carefully.

> **Remember: any *area of provision can have* any *focus when there is an adult in it to direct the learning, so* always think continuous provision when there is no adult there in a teaching role.**

This might also help you to generate a list of resources that you can beg, steal, borrow or buy to help you to meet the needs of your children. The great thing about that is that when you then hand in a list of resources to be signed off, everything you have identified has been linked directly to assessment and doesn't look like you just picked it out of the catalogue because you fancied the look of it.

When you and your team start thinking about assessment in this 'broad sweep' way it can really focus your judgements and help to create a greater team coherence. If you are using tools such as GSA to help you to plan your space, then you are already able to demonstrate to anyone who wants to know that your environment is linked to assessment and has been structured to support the needs of all children (even the most able!).

Don't think of continuous provision as the provision that is continuously available for the children. Think of it as resources that you have put out that will continue the provision for learning in the absence of an adult. Ask yourself the question: how does the construction area that you have set up have the potential to continue the provision for your children's learning when there is no adult there? That doesn't mean telling all of the children they have to build a tower taller than 15 bricks – that is an adult-directed challenge.

The best way to ensure true continuous provision is to look at skill development, which we will do in this chapter, and follow this with effective planning (see Chapter 5, p.55). Also, pop into your EYFS department once they have all gone home and see if they have got copies of *Continuous Provision in the Early Years* and *Continuous Provision: The Skills*. If they do, nick them! Also have a look in their stock cupboard – I bet they have got some sparkly pipe cleaners hidden at the back for a rainy day! *So, that's where the art budget went!*

Keep 'topic' as an enhancement only!

Your continuous provision is the backbone of your space; it is linked to children's skill and experiential development. Your continuous provision should *not* be completely themed around topic or activity as then it ceases to become continuous provision and becomes an adult-initiated activity. If you are talking about shape and then you put shapes in your water tray – and nothing else – this isn't continuous provision for water play, it is a shape activity in the water. Provision to develop the *skills* of water play would be to have continuous provision for water play in place and then you might add some objects with interesting shapes as an enhancement. The shapes would not be the only thing the children could play with or the thing the children *had* to play with, but something they could choose to play with and interpret in their own way. This sort of enhancement gives adults the opportunity to use the language of shape in water play rather than force an activity on children who don't want to do it.

If you ask all of the children to make a hedgehog out of dough in your malleable materials area, this is not continuous provision. It might be autumn, and you might be talking about hedgehogs and you might have been onto Pinterest and seen some really cute dough ones, but we should be planning for skill development and process not just outcome. You may be planning to develop your children's fine motor dexterity in your malleable materials area, so you would provide them with lots of opportunities to pinch, pull and roll as part of your continuous provision. This could be making an alien, spider man, a tank – whatever takes their fancy. As you have been talking about hedgehogs, you might enhance your malleable materials with some images of hedgehogs and some resources that would support children if they wanted to make a hedgehog. But there should be no sign saying 'Can you make a hedgehog?'. More often than not the answer would be: 'Yes, but I don't want to thanks. Can I make a sea monster?'.

Areas to avoid in continuous provision

The following I would avoid anyway, but especially when you are tight on space! I would not have (in Year One, or EYFS for that matter) a writing area, mathematics area or reading area. What? The Holy Trinity of attainment? Yes! Why?

Writing

As anyone who is a regular reader of my blog will know, I am very passionate about getting children writing (especially boys). Over the past few years I have done lots of project work on improving mark making and writing across a variety of settings. I spend lots of my time thinking about, and watching, what motivates children to want to mark make and write.

Undoubtedly, as in all things, motivation is the key. If children aren't motivated to write, then they won't do it. Often things that we think are a great idea as a writing inspiration don't catch children's imagination and therefore they are not bothered (usually finding that they need to do a poo just about the time you want them to write! It is an old trick, but it always works – who amongst us is going to take the risk of saying 'no' to an oncoming and urgent poo!).

A topic-based approach to learning can often cause disengagement when it comes to writing as opposed to a child-led approach which usually results in a high level of interest. Well, what is my brilliant idea for the writing area? Simple – get rid of it. I know it sounds a bit drastic and some of you might have even given out an audible gasp as you read the last sentence, but from what I have seen across *all* of the settings I have done this with, it makes perfect sense and produces some amazing results.

Removing any explicit area is not something that you should do without some consideration and evaluation. So, the first question I usually ask when we are thinking about a 'writing area extraction' is, 'What can you do in the mark making/writing area that you cannot do anywhere else in your setting?'. (So far, no one has come up with an answer.)

The thing about having a mark making area is that you are making it a 'destination activity'. If you are thinking about paint or construction, then it makes more sense to have an area or areas to go to build or create. But with basic skills, you want children to practise them everywhere. They should be part of what you do in *every* area not something that you have to go to a specific place to 'do'. Of course, if you are not keen on writing or not very good at it then you will just avoid that destination, heading instead for construction or the scooters! If there was a range of mark making resources in the construction area and outside with the scooters, then you would be far more likely to use them. Even if you weren't rushing to pick them up, any adult playing/working with you would have far more opportunity to get you writing on the spot than they would if they had to say, 'How about we go to the mark making area and…'. The flip side of that – and I see this an *awful* lot – is that children who do like to mark make and write find themselves in the writing area for long periods of time on a very regular basis, often having a lovely time producing the same sort of mark making again and again. Although children feeling accomplishment and success in a skill is brilliant for their self-esteem and wellbeing (and should be encouraged), we also need to consider what those children are actually doing at the writing table (again) and how we can promote their self-esteem while also taking their learning and experience forward.

If you are a reluctant writer and you are inspired to do a bit one day, you might be disappointed when you make it to the mark making/writing area to find that it is already full of children who can write! What am I suggesting? In the first instance, you need to observe your writing area. This is best done several times a day over a period of time, especially during periods of continuous provision. Who is in your writing area and what are they doing? More importantly, who isn't in your writing area and what are they doing? Usually a profile quickly emerges of those that do and those that don't.

Next, think about your other areas of provision. How many of them contain opportunities to write? Not just a clipboard and a pile of A4 paper in the construction area; do you have little books, scrapbooks, a small range of writing materials and prompts for writing in every area? I have seen prolific mark making as part of sand and water play and exploration, albeit slightly soggy at times!

Have you got mobile mark making stations or carriers containing mark making resources such as pencils, felt tips, etc.? Everything from your humble Pringles tube covered in wrapping paper to a cutlery drainer will work. You can personalise carriers for individual

children meaning that everyone (or just key children) has their own to take wherever they go. I have recently done some work using cardboard wine carriers that were personalised by the children – they worked really well.

In most Year One settings, space is at a premium and the explicit areas of provision that you create should link directly to your summative assessment, as this tells you what your children need most in terms of support and challenge. If we make writing an explicit area, we are discouraging children from seeing it as an integral part of their play and learning. In all of the settings where we have taken away the 'writing area' and put writing opportunities in all areas and then assessed the results, we have seen no change at all in the mark making and writing of the children who were regulars in the writing area. Where we have seen the biggest change is with the children who never went near the writing area. Their engagement with mark making and writing significantly improved overnight and that engagement was sustained. Staff also reported a huge increase in the number of opportunities for mark making and writing through play that presented themselves.

For me, when it comes to 'basic skills' in Early Years and Year One, I consistently see the biggest successes with children's engagement and learning when those skills are implicit not explicit. So, there are lots of opportunities to use literacy and numeracy as part of play and not as an add on.

Mathematics and reading

I would urge you to look at your mathematics and reading areas in the same way as your writing area. I rarely see children in mathematics areas actually doing maths in the absence of an adult, whereas I see lots of practical maths experiences going on in continuous provision when areas are enhanced with mathematics resources. Mathematics areas are more often than not empty or used by children for role play.

When it comes to reading areas, how often do you see your reading area full of children reading? Children tend to like to read on their own or in twos and threes, not in groups of six or eight. I observe more exploring of books and reading happening where children have small spaces to go and read in.

Think about creating a 'book nook' in your space rather than a large reading space that you will find gets used for role play or messing about! Also add some baskets of books to all of your areas of provision, so that adults and children can use them in their play and exploration.

Add in a bit of ambiguity

Although you want some structure to support you in the planning of your environment, what you don't want is an over-planned space where *everything* is linked to 'topic', literacy or numeracy. Children are more likely to engage when the play is based around their current interests. They also need lots of open-ended opportunities to explore and investigate, so make sure you have lots of ambiguous open-ended resources to promote learning.

Common play behaviours

As discussed at the start of the chapter, good continuous provision in Year One can be tricky – all too often children will just visit an area of provision that they like, where they will choose a resource that they are familiar with and then engage in low-level tasks, often for a considerable period of time. This is great for their levels of engagement, but not so much for their levels of progress or attainment.

Of course, we want children to be happy – happy children make successful learners! But we also want children to be motivated and challenged by the resources that we provide for them. We want them to be thinkers, negotiators and problem solvers – to apply the knowledge that they already have to enable them to explore new possibilities. When your children are in front of you and hanging on your every word, you (the skillful adult) can impart, tease and celebrate knowledge and achievement. But when they go into continuous provision, it is the environment that you provide that needs to do that job – almost as well as you do (and in some cases better).

The following method is one that I use with lots of Early Years settings and Year One classrooms that they find straightforward to apply as a starting point to their provision.

Common play behaviours for effective continuous provision

In order to establish a good base for effective continuous provision, we need to appreciate children's common play behaviours. In Chapter 2 (p.13), I discussed using the GSA to identify where the biggest gaps in children's learning are and also where children are performing above the expected level of development for their age, then using this information to help decide which areas of provision to create or highlight within the learning space.

Remember, there is no law that says you must have a certain area. You can have a number of 'exclusive' areas of provision or you could have none depending on the needs of your children. A jigsaw table is not a statutory requirement! Children will also move resources that you have provided in one area to utilise in their play elsewhere. This is okay. The more fluid you can make your environment, the more opportunities for learning there will be. The data that you gather and the observations that you make will guide you towards the areas of provision that you decide to create, but only by taking the time to monitor them will tell you if they are successful or not – that is why there is no writing table, mathematics area or reading corner for me!

Each area of provision that you create needs a variety of interesting and stimulating resources that engage children and have the potential to extend their learning. Continuous provision has to continue the provision for learning in the absence of an adult and that is where the crucial difference lies. If, for example, your GSA has indicated that there are lots of skills and experiences that your children would gain through sand play and exploration, I would suggest you create a sand area. But what are you going to put on the shelves? More importantly, why are you putting it there? This is where the concept of common play behaviours comes in…

1. Identify common play behaviours

I want children to be able to play, explore, investigate and interpret in ways that are personal to them so I am not saying that they can *only* use the resources that I provide in the way that I intend them to be used. What I am saying is: 'I know what you *usually* do in the sand when there is no adult. So, I am going to provide resources that will support and challenge that common play behaviour.'

The first thing I would ask you and/or your team to do would be to identify common play behaviours of children in the sand tray. If this is not very familiar to you as a Year One practitioner, then you need to call on your Early Years team to help you. If you are a very lucky Year One practitioner, then your Early Years team will already have a common play behaviours format in place and they will be passing it all on to you during transition with the progression already in place.

If you haven't got lots of EYFS experience and your EYFS team hasn't already got common play behaviours in place, then you can take each area of provision that you have created and, over a period of time, observe children in play – not with any sort of direct challenge, just in free play. You can then write down the sort of play that you see. Some areas like sand have a number of common play behaviours; we would end up with a list that would look something like this:

- dig
- pour
- fill
- empty
- mark make
- mould/manipulate
- enclose/bury
- transport
- cause and effect.

… plus any more that you can think of. (There are also lots of opportunity for discussion about how some of the common play behaviours are linked and cross over with each other.)

I am always careful to make sure that the common play behaviours are linked to sand itself, rather than enhancements to sand play like small world. The enhancements will be added into your continuous provision in response to children's interests; they would be things that you are introducing to the children, or investigating with the children, such as skills or specific challenges.

2. Implicitly level each common play behaviour

I usually then transfer these common play behaviours to a simple A4 grid. At this point in the process we are going to implicitly level each common play behaviour that you have identified. We will do this over three broad levels: emergent, mid-level and high-level. The word 'level' can be easily misconstrued by some and conjures up thoughts of 'top shelf, middle shelf, bottom shelf' and children being told to only use the resources on their allotted shelf. This is absolutely *not* what we are aiming for! The term 'implicit levelling' means exactly that – it is implied. You know that it is there, but to the children it just looks like a collection of interesting resources for them to experiment with. If the term 'levelling' scares you or someone close to you, then you can always just refer to it as differentiation – it is basically the same thing!

First on our list of common play behaviours in sand is 'dig'. So, what would an emergent digger use to dig with? What sort of space would they need? Is the sand tray on the floor or at waist height? Would the sand be wet or dry? Would it always be sand? (Add to this any other questions you or your team generate.) An emergent digger is likely to start to dig with their hand. After their hand, what might they use next? In my experience it is usually a container that is easy to manipulate and after that, probably a scoop.

Your list of tools for an emergent digger *might* go something like:

- hand
- container
- scoop.

When you are thinking about a mid-level digger, they might access tools such as

- spade (short handle)
- spade (long handle)
- serving spoon (large)
- ladle
- wooden spoon (large)
- spatula.

And a higher level digger? Well, something like:

- wooden spoon (small)
- small scoop
- teaspoon
- fingers
- lollipop sticks
- something with a mechanism
- non-specified resources of their own invention!

Of course, all of the challenge for digging does not come from the size of the utensil. There will be challenge from the size of the digging area, the texture of what they are digging in, etc. For the purposes of this exercise we are thinking about shelves next to an indoor sand tray. It is not an exact science nor is this an exhaustive list, but hopefully it will illustrate the process. Once I have done this for digging, I would then apply the same process to pouring, filling and emptying and so on. When my common play behaviours for sand grid is complete, I would then move on to all of the other areas of provision that I had created and do a grid for those areas too.

You can re-use these grids, just add or adjust for different cohorts. Figure 4 (p.38) shows an example of how to fill in a common play behaviours grid for sand. This grid is not complete – some of the sections are empty or incomplete – but it should give you the idea. You would need to add more columns as not all of the common play behaviours have been recorded.

3. Customising for your cohort

For the purposes of transition, your Reception cohort's common play behaviours overview will give you a clear outline of the sort of resources you need to provide to maintain and extend your children's skill level in every area of provision.

As a Year One teacher, I might think that I am going to establish a sand tray in my classroom, but what often happens is that I then have to go hunting for resources from the back of the stock cupboard and what I end up putting out is all that I can find. If I put out some buckets and scoops and a couple of large funnels for my Year One children, then my common play behaviours for sand document would show me that, in terms of skill development, what I had put out for my children was fairly emergent – the sort of resource that children would encounter very early on in their experience of sand play. This in turn would no doubt give me high levels of engagement because building a sandcastle with a scoop and a bucket is easy. But it is unlikely to challenge children in the development of their skills and overall learning. If anything it will cause that learning to stagnate, resulting in low levels of attainment and progress. So, I look at each column on my common play behaviours for sand document and then apply what is on them to my children. Do I have any emergent diggers?

- Yes I do – I know the sort of resource that I need to put out.
- No I don't – I need to move on to a more challenging digging resource for their continuous progression.

If I have emergent, mid-level and high-level diggers, then I need a bit of everything. This is not prescriptive nor exhaustive, this is a continuous provision skeleton that you can build on and enhance.

Some of the most effective continuous provision I have seen will have resources that support *all* of the common play behaviours identified within that area available for the children, plus some quality enhancements.

What adults *must not* do is to go into a space and say: 'You're a high-level digger, so drop the scoop and pick up the teaspoon… or else!'. We have to be appreciative of the subtleties of children's play and seek to understand *their* interpretations and explanations, which often don't match our assumptions and are rarely black and white! Children need a variety of resources and the freedom to experiment with them, underpinned by the adult's knowledge and rigour of the provision.

What you have got with a common play behaviours approach is a scaffold for learning that is based on assessment and development and which supports children in their exploration of process and skill either with or without an adult. I would tweak my resources in response to observation, and every time I did a summative assessment I would reassess my provision against my common play behaviours format, then add my enhancements.

Skill development

As I have already mentioned, we need to ensure that children have a high level of engagement in their play, but also that we are providing an environment and provision that not only consolidates their knowledge, but also promotes the application of it. A skills-based approach to planning encourages us to think about how we can do this through skill development rather than just activity or enhancement.

Pure and facilitative skills and experiences

The first thing that you have to do in each and every area of provision is to identify which are the 'pure' skills and experiences that the area offers, and which skills and experiences are 'facilitative'.

Continuous Provision: Common Play Behaviours

			AREA: SAND			
Behaviour	Dig	Pour	Fill and Empty	Mould	Mould Tools	Sieve and Sift
HIGH-LEVEL	Fingers Small scoop Teaspoon Tablespoon Dessert spoon	Small vessel with side handle Large vessel (heavy) Vessel with tap Smaller vessel, no handle, no spout Large vessel, no handle, no spout	As Dig and Pour	Fingers Self-made moulds Small natural materials Small irregular shapes Small regular shapes	Fingers Small scoop Teaspoon Tablespoon Dessert spoon	Fingers Fabric (small weave) Comb Tea leaf straining spoon Tea strainer
MID-LEVEL	Spatula Wooden spoon Slotted spoon Serving spoon Long-handled spade Short-handled spade	Pouring vessel, long spout Small vessel (irregular) Small vessel (tall) Large vessel (irregular) Large vessel (tall)		Smaller irregular shape Large irregular shape Smaller tall container Large taller container	Fingers Small scoop Teaspoon Tablespoon Dessert spoon	Potato masher Mesh sieve (small) Mesh sieve (large) Sieve (small hole) Sieve (large hole)
EMERGENT	Scoop Smaller regular container Large regular container (hard)	Smaller vessel, no handle Large vessel, no handle Smaller vessel with handle Large vessel with handle and defined spout		Smaller regular container (bucket) Large regular container Hand	Scoop Smaller regular container Large regular container Hand	Fabric (large weave) Colander Grain sifter Fingers

Figure 4: Compiling the common play behaviours for sand.

- **Pure skills or experiences** – children will *only* be able to experience these through that area
- **Facilitative skills or experiences** – children will be able to experience these through a number of areas.

The pure skills and experiences are usually the most basic ones, and they need to be experienced and mastered first by children. It is only when they have a good knowledge of the pure skills and experiences that they can apply that knowledge to other learning.

As previously noted, two of the main areas of stagnation in any Year One classroom are the sand and the water. More often than not, children will enjoy playing in those areas, but they will resort to very low-level skills and experiences because they can, they are familiar and they are easy. How many children do you see who just stand at the water tray and pour. Pouring is great fun, but it also features at 16–26 months in the *Early Years Outcomes*, so at its basic level, it is not the most taxing!

If we take the good old sand tray as an example, what we need to do is to identify the pure skills and experiences that you can get from the sand tray and then identify the teaching and learning opportunities that you can facilitate through the sand tray. By doing this, we can ensure we are planning provision that actually meets the needs of our children.

When I am carrying out this exercise with a setting, we usually take a large piece of flip-chart paper and write the areas we are focusing on at the top (in this case 'sand') and then split the page into two halves: 'pure' and 'facilitative'. I would then ask the team to fill in each column. They will know it is a pure skill or experience if they cannot do it in any other area of provision. 'Digging', for example, would go under the 'facilitative' heading because you can dig in areas other than sand.

Sand	
Pure	Facilitative
Unique properties of sand (wet and dry)	Digging Sifting Enclosing Pattern making Construction Magnetism Cause and effect Imprinting Moulding

Figure 5: Pure and facilitative skills and experiences.

Warning: This will make your brain ache, but it is a good ache and it will really help you when it comes to planning for your environment and tracking attainment.

Most teams will find creating a facilitative list of skills and experiences significantly easier than the pure list. The list in Figure 5 is not exhaustive for the facilitative skills and experiences, but it will give you the idea. There is only one pure skill/experience.

There are some areas of provision that have no pure skills or experiences. Construction is one of them. There is nothing that you can do in the construction area that you can't do somewhere else; build, stack, bridge, join are all very transferrable skills. We are often tempted by a construction area in Year One, as it can be perceived to be the 'key' to engaging those more difficult to engage children (often, but not always, the boys!). Unless we are looking at a method of planning a construction area that develops skills, we run the risk of providing construction kits that require a low level of skill. This can result in a high level of engagement, because it is easy, but a low level of potential for progress or attainment, because there is limited challenge – if any.

Construction has loads of facilitative skills, such as:

- promotes learning about the function of objects, entrances, exits and pathways and how to navigate inside, out, through and round
- allows children to show their knowledge of something and how it works long before they have the language to be able to verbalise what it is they know
- supports fine and gross motor development
- encourages the development of spacial awareness
- enables children to collect information through observation
- helps children to classify by common characteristics
- allows children to explore what happens to an object as you manipulate it
- explores trajectory (commonly known as chucking or dropping your blocks!)
- promotes finding out how weight and shape effects movement and motion (it is much harder to roll a square brick than a round one!)
- allows children to explore force and motion
- enables children to experience height, width, length and size
- gives children the opportunity to sort, count, make patterns, sequence, remember numbers, count on, work with fractions (construction kits like Duplo™ and Lego™ are particularly good for this)
- enables children to use geometric shapes with a 'real' purpose
- enables children to create symmetry
- enables children to experience scale (children need the opportunity to build with large and small construction materials).

Cognitive strategies
Working together in construction encourages:

- empathy
- sharing
- negotionation
- discussion
- acquisition of language (especially through peer building projects).

Construction allows children to practise:

- grouping
- stacking
- ramping
- creating lines
- covering
- bridging
- enclosing (when making tunnels or houses)
- making things equal
- balance
- creating shapes
- stepping (as in making steps)
- stability.

Admittedly, lots of the above are easily developed by construction kits and it makes sense to have one area that primarily develops them, but none of them are exclusive. If children are not choosing to come into an area because they are not interested in it or motivated by it, we can actively ensure that they are getting access to those skills elsewhere.

Role play
If we look at role play as an example of an area of provision where talk skills can be promoted and explored, there are loads of talk skills that children could potentially develop through their play and interaction. Please note there are no pure skills for role play – all of the skills that you develop in the role play area can be developed elsewhere too, such as in small world and anywhere else that children gather to role play together. Here's a broad overview of some of skills that role play offers:

Facilitative skills and experiences

- Development of pretence – children developing the capacity to use their imagination to feed their play.
- Development and use of receptive and expressive language – children's ability to listen to and understand what is being said to them and also their ability to communicate their ideas and thoughts in a way that others can understand.
- Mental representations – ideas that children create in their mind and then play out through role play.
- Transform objects – children use their imagination to turn one object into another. The more ambiguous the object, the easier the process. So a box can be a boat, a house, a microwave, a shoe etc.
- Symbolic action – children imagine how something might 'be' or 'feel' and then use this as a mechanism for their play.
- Interactive dialogue – children talk to others who respond appropriately.
- Negotiation – using language and conversation skills to reach a compromise or end result.
- Role taking through choice – children co-operate in play but decide on the role within that play that they would like to take.
- Role taking under direction (co-operation) – children co-operate in play but are happy to be directed by another child or adult who is leading the scenario.
- Improvisation – children have no set or fixed plan for how their play will develop. The scenario emerges as a result of the children's interactions.

Cognitive strategies:

- Joint planning – children work together to come up with a plan.
- Negotiation – joint discussions that lead to an agreed end result.
- Problem solving – taking time to think together or alone to solve a problem or issue.
- Goal seeking – children will work individually or in collaboration to seek an end result.
- Emotion – children can explore a range of emotions in a safe and supported environment.
- Cognition – children acquire new knowledge through language, interaction and experience.
- Language – children can extend their range of vocabulary as well as mechanisms for using and expressing language.
- Sensory motor actions – children make sense of the world through their senses and physical actions.

- Abstract thinking – thinking about the world around them in a different way. For good abstract thinking, children need to be able to use and apply their prior knowledge uniquely.
- Explicit rules – children learn about explicit rules like playing fairly and sharing.
- Implicit rules – children learn about more complex and subtle rules that exist with play like engaging others in their play and maintaining fantasy play, even though they know that it is not 'real'.

Implicit levelling of your skills and experiences

Once you have identified which facilitative skill and experience that you are going to enhance your provision with, then you need to level (differentiate) that skill according to the development level of your children, as you did with the common play behaviours (see Figure 4, p.38). If you have got a broad range of abilities, you will need a range of resources; if you have a much narrower ability spread, then your resource provision might be more focused. For each skill and experience, break it down into levels of complexity – three levels is usually enough, e.g. emergent, developing, advanced.

If I was working with you or your team, we would get out a big sheet of paper and work through the skill/experience development from basic through to advanced. As an example, let's look at the skill of printing:

Emergent skill

Q – What is the most emergent way that children usually create a print?

A – They do it using a flat hand.

Q – Once children progress beyond using their hand (or other body parts!), what might they use that will make printing simple?

A – Found objects with an easy grip or a large surface area like a sponge or leaf.

Q – How might children represent their prints?

A – Single colour, easy application such as paint in a tray or applied with large brush.

Developing skill

Q – Once they have progressed from single prints, how might children develop their skills?

A – First using repeated patterns, random or organised with a single object, then moving on to using repeated patterns, random or organised with a range of objects.

Q – Can you describe what those objects might look like? What characteristics make them harder/easier to use?

A – The objects would probably still have a large surface area to make them easy to handle. It would be good to provide a variety of textures so that children could begin to appreciate the different print effects that they could create.

Advanced skill

Q – How can I make printing even more challenging?

A – Items that the children print with can become more challenging in terms of the dexterity that is needed to manipulate them. The children can also be challenged by employing different printing techniques such as relief printing and imprinting. Children will also be able to explore other concepts like colour mixing through their development of printing.

An initial hierarchy for the skill of 'printing' might look something like this:

- Random experimental printing with hands, feet and found materials.
- Explores both relief printing and imprinting (in materials like dough and clay).
- Uses one colour of paint on a block or in a tray.
- Makes repeating patterns, random or organised, with a range of large blocks or objects that are easy to manipulate (including handles like pan scrubs, etc.).
- Explores a variety of tools to apply paint to printing object.
- Explores repeated pattern with one colour and one object or by imprinting with one object.
- Extends repeating patterns – overlapping, using two contrasting colours, using different objects.
- Explores and recreates patterns and textures with an extended range of materials, e.g. sponges, leaves, fruit.
- Explores images through relief printing on a variety of papers.
- Uses a wide variety of tools that become more challenging in dexterity to produce the image, to take a relief print of or to use to create an imprint.
- Explores images and recreates texture using a variety of found objects, e.g. wallpaper, string, polystyrene.
- Explores colour mixing through printing, using two colours and a variety of materials.
- Explores layering of prints to create effect.
- Uses printing to represent the natural environment.
- Uses the work of a well-known artist as a provocation for printing and pattern making.
- Recreates images through relief printing using fine motor tools.
- Recreates a scene remembered, observed or imagined, through collage printing.
- Creates prints for a purpose, e.g. fabric, book covers and wallpaper.

Once you have identified the skill you are going to be focusing on and then broken that skill down into its levels of development, you then match those levels to the children that you have got. If you have got no children at the emergent stage of development, then you wouldn't put out the low-level resources in your creative provision. By the same token, if you have got no children at the higher level of development, then you wouldn't put any of those resources out.

Implicit levelling is everywhere in your classroom space from the scissor pot to glue. What do you mean, how do you level glue? Just apply the same principle: emergent, developing, advanced. What is the most **emergent** gluing resource that we give children? – A glue stick. (You might give them PVA to swirl about, but in terms of actually glueing something for a purpose, you probably want a glue stick). When children's experience and dexterity is **developing** beyond a glue stick, what comes next? Usually PVA. You can even level within PVA: What makes it easiest to apply? – Finger. Then what? – Brush. Then? – Plastic glue spreader or cotton bud. Why? – Because they both require more dexterity and are harder to manipulate. What about after that? – Well, it is not superglue. That could be disastrous! It is not about the strength of the glue, it is about the complexity of the skill. So what would take more skill and process? Paste! You can provide children with a sugar shaker full of flour and a dispenser of water and get them to mix their own, or give them wallpaper paste and water and encourage them to mix the two.

Labelling and dressing for interest

Once you are confident that your environment has got a firm foundation built on assessment and that you have implicitly levelled the resources that you have put on your shelves, linking them to skills progression as well as children's interest, then you can start thinking about labelling and dressing those spaces for interest. When I refer to 'labelling', I am using it in the broadest sense of the word, so enhancing a space with images, text, photographs, etc. 'Dressing' is taking a specific interest of the child, this could be superheroes, princesses, spiders or anything they are passionate about, then adding elements of this interest into the environment or specific resource.

It is important to remember that you are labelling and dressing for interest and not for gender. It may be that you have got a group of children who love dinosaurs, who happen to be boys, or a group of children that love princesses that happen to be girls. But when you are thinking about dressing or enhancing your space you are thinking about their interest regardless of their gender.

By the very nature of a play-based environment, children are going to use it to play in! I have talked a lot about wanting children to be able to be able to explore their space, use ambiguous open-ended resources and develop a skill-based approach to learning. Well, often the result of that is a bit of 'active mess'. Active mess is very different to your space being well and truly trashed. Trash usually happens when children lack some direction in their learning or when the adults are not present in the play with the children to help to support their learning, and then also reset the learning spaces.

There are a few ways you can tackle this, although when you have got large numbers of children exploring your environment, nothing is guaranteed!

- Direct challenge – this will be discussed in Chapter 5 (p.61)
- 'Dressing' specific resources, or even areas of provision, for interest.

Dressing for interest

If you have a group of fine motor children (who may be girls) who are into princesses and a group of more gross motor children (who may be boys) who are into dinosaurs, then you could create two boxes of resources: one that contains lots of things that challenge and develop fine motor skills and another that challenge and develop more gross motor skills.

If I just put these two boxes in my environment, then the target group of children do stand a higher chance of coming into the space and accessing some resources that will take their learning forward. But, if I 'dress' the fine motor resources and the box in a princess theme and the gross motor in a dinosaur theme, then my gross motor target children are more likely to come into the area in the first place because there is a dinosaur box in there. When the children get in there, they are more likely to put their hands in the dinosaur box than the princess one. Therefore they are significantly more likely to be accessing a resource that has been specifically chosen to help their development. You cannot guarantee that this will happen every time, but what you can do is say with confidence that you have *maximised* the potential for attainment in continuous provision and *minimised* the risk of failure. Now when anyone asks you if you can quantify attainment outside of focused teaching, the job just got a whole lot easier and as a practitioner, you can be secure in the knowledge that your continuous provision is really continuing the provision for learning and isn't just a collection of lovely resources.

This method of 'dressing' can be very successful but can sometimes be a little bit too generic. It may be that you have a group of children who are all interested in dinosaurs, but whose level of attainment is significantly different. For that group, a box themed around one ability level wouldn't be as effective.

Using the children's images

One very effective way of targeting specific resources is to use the children's images. Small photographs stuck onto wooden pegs works well. If you have differentiated resources around a particular skill, then you would peg the faces of the children who needed to access a particular range of resources around the basket or box that those resources were in. You can then move the pegs as the children become more proficient and move them and reuse them in other areas.

The role of the adult

Probably the initiative with the most impact in getting children to access levelled resources is us, the adult. For any continuous provision to work, adults *have* to be in it, working and playing alongside children. Continuous provision is considerably more effective when adults are moving through the space and are not tethered to one particular area or activity. The more the adults can move, the more they can provoke, teach and support.

Another ideal, which I know can be difficult, is making sure that all of the adults that are going to be working within your space are aware of how and why it has been set up in the way that it has. The more understanding they have then the more effective they will be within their role. If you have created provision linked to assessment that is levelled and dressed for interest, then all of the adults who are going to work in the space should be aware of what is where and why. This way, when they are moving through your space, they will know what they are looking for and will be able to make accurate assessments as to whether the provision is being correctly accessed. If it isn't or if a child needs support or challenge, they know which resources to use and how to use them.

You might decide that you are going to have three sessions of direct teaching each day (see the timetable template in Chapter 7, p.77). These will be at the beginning or the end of a session of continuous provision as you don't want to compromise the children's opportunities for sustained shared thinking, exploration and deep-level learning.

Take the time to work with your team to really ensure that everyone has an understanding of skill development in children and how effective use of the indoor and outdoor environment can have a significant impact on their attainment. Of course children's development both indoors and out is not purely linked to markers of academic attainment, although the current educational climate puts us under immense pressure to work purely to these academic goals.

One of the great joys about running an Early Years approach to Year One is the opportunity to build children's imagination, language and ability to think creatively. As a practitioner you will be able to promote all of these skills through the activities that you plan and the direct teaching opportunities that you create. But, we should also be ensuring that we are giving children lots of open-ended experiences in their continuous provision that allow them to discover, experiment and explore within the environment around them both inside and out.

Regular assessment of children's life experience, language, talk and thinking skills should be used to help you to enhance your provision with open-ended resources that will help your teaching to have impact on promoting and enhancing these essential skills.

4 Continuing the provision for learning

In Early Years settings there are lots of different types of provision, all of which can exist very successfully in a Year One classroom.

In the last chapter, I introduced 'continuous provision' (p.27), where we are thinking about creating spaces that will engage children and continue the provision for learning in the absence of an adult. What we have to be really wary of is creating spaces with limited low-level resources that encourage children to stagnate in their learning. At the very least this leads to limited opportunities for learning, but often if children remain in this sort of play for long periods of time they become bored and disruptive. Sometimes people will say to me that the children are 'ready for more than play', when actually it is the sort of resources and opportunities that are being offered that are the issue – not the child needing to sit down at a table with a worksheet to gain fulfilment.

The provision pyramid

Figure 6 is a diagram of the 'provision pyramid' – a sort of segmented Toblerone! It is a handy visual aid to look at when we are talking about the different types of provision and where they are appropriate.

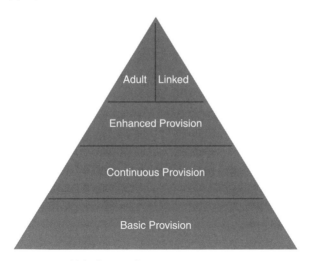

Figure 6: *The provision pyramid (abcdoes.com).*

The wider the triangle, the more organic the play; the narrower it gets, the more adult intervention is taking place. In an ideal world we neither want to spend all of our time at the bottom or the top – just somewhere in the middle.

Basic provision

Basic provision comes at the bottom of the provision pyramid because it is the broadest and simplest provision that we provide for children. You should only really use basic provision on point of entry *if* your Reception team have not provided you with accurate assessment.

At it's most 'basic', basic provision is just putting out in the environment the only resources that you have! In settings that have a range of resources at their disposal, basic provision is the provision of interesting and familiar resources that you provide for children to support transition into your environment, but which is not linked directly to your assessment of their strengths, needs or learning preferences. What you set out for your basic provision is often linked to the general age-related expectations for children.

Once you have carried out your first set of assessments, you can begin to apply that knowledge to your environment and areas of provision that exist within it. At this point you will be moving your provision to the next level on the pyramid – continuous provision.

Continuous provision

Good continuous provision really does raise the potential for attainment and minimise the risk of failure, stagnation or boredom in your environment. As I explained in the previous chapter, it is not just a collection of resources that you put out to keep the children busy or happy once they have finished their work. It is an enabler, a prompt for learning linked to assessment, skill development and engagement.

In any area where you put a range of resources and a group of children there will be potential to develop those children's skills in personal interaction and exploration, but unless those resources have been carefully selected to meet the development needs of those specific children, the learning potential is limited and greatly left to chance. When children are given the opportunity to 'choose', they tend to pick things that they like and know that they can do. If you track your children when they go into continuous provision, you will often find the same children in the same spaces doing the same sort of things day in, day out, week in, week out. The problem is that they often look 'busy' which allows us to get on with the other jobs that we need to do. But are they busy learning or busy doing what they always do and have been doing for the past couple of years?

Often we can also mistake compliance with engagement or attainment and this can be a fatal error. There will be lots of children who are very happy to stay in an area of the provision for sustained periods of time. They will comply to the agreed behaviour code and will often be prolific in their output. But if we look at what they have produced and then ask ourselves if it shows challenge and learning or just low-level consolidation of a skill that they already had then we are far more likely to see that it is the latter. This is another example of where we could be using continuous provision as a holding activity, until an adult gets to them and boosts their attainment with their input. If you are running a system of continuous provision in Year One then your children will spend a large chunk of their time engaged in it every day. If this provision is not having an impact on their learning then we could be in serious trouble! So, if your continuous provision is just a selection of resources linked to a general area of development, then when a child is playing in there, their opportunities for learning are limited.

As well as providing opportunities for exploration and discovery, your continuous provision *has* to be linked to your assessment of your current cohort. If it is going to be available all of the time and children are going to access it with limited adult input, it *has* to be structured around their development needs and dressed to reflect their interests. Could you answer the following questions about your basic continuous provision?

- Have you created your areas of provision based around your GSA (see Chapter 2, p.13)?
- Does the size of your area of continuous provision reflect the needs of your cohort? If you have children who need to develop language and talk skills, have you significantly increased the size of those areas?
- Have you implicitly levelled your continuous provision (see Chapter 3, p.34), linked to assessment so that you can show which resources have been placed in there, linked to the development of high, middle and low achievers in that area?

Enhanced provision

Once you have levelled your provision to make it 'continuous' then you can begin to enhance it to support what you are focusing on in your teaching and learning and the specific interests of your children. Your enhancements are things that you 'add in' to your continuous provision. Most enhancements come from five main sources:

- the theme that you are talking about
- children's interests
- basic skill, area of learning or subject area
- teaching a skill
- explicit challenge.

In some areas, you will have more than one enhancement within a week, while in other areas you might have none. What is important is that you make your enhancements just that – an enhancement – and that they sit alongside good continuous provision.

Linked provision

Linked provision is a daily short session of play-based, child-led activities that have been planned around a specific area of need or consolidation that you have identified through observation and assessment. It is a bit of a hybrid that I first used with a Reception setting to help them to get round their issue of hearing guided readers, without compromising their continuous provision. Since then I have worked on versions of it from Early Years to Year One. Linked provision is by no means an essential part of your day; it is just a strategy that I have used with lots of settings now that has not only solved some timetabling issues, but has had a significant impact on attainment.

I would run linked provision as a daily session – usually at the very beginning of the day. Everyone is engaged in activities that are themed around the identified need. The same activities are repeated every day for a week and the children get to experience and repeat all of them.

I have worked with settings that have used linked provision in a variety of ways, such as:

- to reinforce teaching and concepts from the week before
- to support social development, with lots of activities that involve turn-taking or sharing
- as a designated talk time, where the children have been encouraged to work in large or small groups around particular aspects of talk
- to teach new concepts that will then be made available in continuous provision, so children learn how to play games like dominoes or lotto
- to support fine and gross motor skill development
- to focus on problem solving or thinking skills
- to work on number recognition, number bonds, shape or measure.

A session of linked provision lasts anything between 10 and 20 minutes depending on the age of the children and their stage of development. Like continuous provision, linked provision *must* be activity based, child-led, active and fun. Linked provision is *not* sitting down at a table with a handwriting sheet, or sitting on the carpet with a whiteboard and pen. It is active and engaging!

During a session of linked provision, I wouldn't make all areas available. Ideally this would be great, but realistically it is just too difficult to manage and maintain. I would set up 'key' areas or 'stations' that were linked to the subject you are focusing on and let the children work in those.

What is the role of the adult in linked provision?

The role of the adult may change depending on the focus, but primarily they are there to facilitate, teach and support quality learning through play. In some settings, each adult manages an 'activity' or 'area', especially when the link is to something like the rules of game play. Sometimes one adult has taken an overview of the provision while the other adult, or adults, have withdrawn children for interventions like speech and language support. This is also a really good time for hearing children read, rather than during playtime or the afternoon session.

If you pull a child out of good continuous provision, then you run a great risk of compromising their learning – the provision isn't continuous if you keep stopping it. Because linked provision is a much shorter session, themed around a more specific focus and repeated across the week, children have multiple opportunities to revisit a concept in a variety of contexts.

I would always have my linked provision sessions first thing, following self-registration. This also allows time for any late-comers who then don't miss out on any direct input. At the end of linked provision, I would then come to the carpet for a good old talk session, signposting of the day or a direct teaching session.

Adult-led provision

Adult-led provision is when an adult goes into the provision, rather than taking children out of it. As soon as you engage with children in continuous provision, the play becomes at least 'adult influenced' if not adult led.

Adult-led provision can have a very positive impact on children's engagement and attainment if done sensitively. It can also be very effective at sending learning off the rails and scattering children to the four corners of your setting (especially if you have a clipboard in your hand). Judging if, when and how you intervene in children's play is not an exact science and no one gets it right all of the time. But, when you do it well, it allows you to observe, challenge, support and extend children's learning all based on the high-level engagement that you will get because they are at play.

5 Planning for continuous provision

Alongside your planning for your direct teaching, whether that be whole class, group or one-to-one, you need to produce a separate plan for your continuous provision. It is really important that your continuous provision planning is as rigorous as your input for sessions like phonics or maths. This plan does not need to be complex, it just needs to outline the areas you are planning specific enhancements for, what those enhancements are and the sort of learning you hope they will promote.

One issue that often arises when we do our continuous provision planning is that children don't actually do what we write on the plan. So, the key question to ask yourself when you are planning is, 'Will they do this when I am not there?'. If the answer is 'no' or, 'probably not', then you need to think again. For example, lots of settings will put specific phonics objectives into their sand or water play continuous provision planning. One setting I worked with had put medial vowel phoneme blends on a ping-pong ball and floated them in their water tray as an 'enhancement'. On their plan they wrote that the children would come to the water, pick out a ping-pong ball and use their knowledge of phonics to create words based on the medial vowel phoneme blend that they chose. In truth, during a session of continuous provision without an adult, this is highly unlikely! Those statements are not continuous provision plans, they are adult focuses within an area of continuous provision – the focus you might want an adult to have when they visit children in play *if* they feel that the play they are observing would benefit from support, challenge or enhancement.

There will also be times when specific areas of continuous provision have been enhanced with a skill that you are focusing on or that contain an explicit challenge for the children to complete, for example you might have enhanced your workshop area with the skill of joining, or used your construction area to facilitate language development. You don't need to write reams and reams of planning to illustrate this really effectively, but there are a few key components that you need to get in there – a good example plan is shown in Figure 7.

I have seen lots of settings create adult prompt cards that differentiate any particular skill focus that they have chosen to enhance an area of continuous provision with. There are many and various ways of doing this; I have seen some settings use the 'WALT' and 'WILF' format for prompt cards for children. What I don't see very often (at all) are children in EYFS or on entry to Year One using 'WALT' and 'WILF' to plan and evaluate their play and learning. If you are going to use prompt cards, then remember to audit their impact through observation. You don't want to spend your life creating laminated cards that no one reads!

Example plan for continuous provision in Year One

Here is an example of a teacher's continuous provision planning for Year One. They have already established the backbone of their continuous provision using a GSA (see Chapter 2, p.13) and they have created a common play behaviours format for all of the areas of provision that they have created (see Chapter 3, p.32).

Continuous Provision Areas & Enhancements Year 1 Autumn I			
Linked Provision - Problem Solving			
Area of Provision	**AOL – Differentiated Objectives**	**Planned Enhancements/Continuous Provision**	**Key Questions**
Sand	**Maths 40–60** **Counts objects to 10 & beyond.** ELG – Children count reliably with numbers from one to 20, place them in order and say which number is one more or one less than a given number. Using quantities and objects, they add and subtract two single-digit numbers and count on or back to find the answer.	**Stones, conkers, sycamore keys, spiders** **Link/Source – Theme & Basic Skills** **Why?** I To develop fine motor skills. I To use language linked to theme. I Engage in Small World play. A To develop counting. A To develop making sets for a number. A To assess concept of adding and subtracting two single digit numbers.	How many? How many more to make …? Which has more/most/ fewest?
Workshop	**Being Imaginative 40-60** **Create simple representations of events, people and objects.** ELO – Children use what they have learnt about media and materials in original ways, thinking about uses and purposes.	**Stippling brushes, paint trays, paint blocks, variety of paper (size and texture). Picture prompts** **Link/Source – BI, Skill and Interest** **Why?** I Experiment with new media. I Self-select. I Talk discuss and interact. A Demonstrate the technique of stippling. A Relate technique to creating texture such as fur or hair. A Language development and encourage co-operation.	What does it look like? How much paint do you need? What does it make you think of?

Figure 7: *Continuous provision areas and enhancements Year 1 Autumn 1.*

In this particular school, the teacher only records the area where they have added enhancements. In the example shown there are only two areas listed. In the whole planning sheet there were seven enhancements in total.

Area of provision

In the left-hand column the teacher has recorded the area of provision in her Year One classroom that the enhancement is going to be added into. In the first example we see they are adding something into their sand area (on top of the continuous provision). In the second, the enhancement is going into their 'workshop' or creative area.

Area of learning

In the second column the teacher has recorded which area of learning the enhancement comes from. In first example mathematics, in the second example 'being imaginative'.

If you had children who had begun the National Curriculum, then you could easily insert subject headings into that box. Here the teacher has differentiated with statements from the *Early Years Outcomes*.

Planned enhancements

The third column is a little more detailed. In this column you would record the following:

- a list of what you had added – the actual resources
- the link or source of the enhancement
- why you are adding in this enhancement to your provision.

I encourage people to write the link or the source of their enhancement. As I mentioned before these *usually* come from one or more of the following:

- the theme that you are talking about
- children's interests
- basic skill, area of learning or subject area
- teaching a skill
- explicit challenge.

In the first example the teacher has recorded 'theme' and 'basic skills'. As it is the beginning of the Autumn term, the theme they are talking about is Autumn and so they have added Autumn resources. They have also recorded basic skills because they would like to encourage the children to use those Autumn resources to support their mathematical development.

The next section they have added to their planning box is 'why'. This is really useful, not only to get it straight in your head, but it also helps any other members of your team who are accessing your planning to have a better understanding of what you are doing – not to mention anyone who might be looking at your planning who is not familiar with Early Years!

This list falls into two sections 'I' for independent and 'A' for adult. I talked earlier about not writing continuous provision plans with unrealistic expectations of what children will do with the resources when there is no adult. In the first box, the adult had added various autumn resources like conkers for sorting, grouping, counting, adding more and taking away. It is very unlikely that a child unprompted will go into the sand tray in an effort to achieve those objectives. That is why under 'I', I would encourage you to give a couple of short examples that illustrate that you understand what a child *might* do with those resources in the absence of an adult. It is only a 'might' not a 'will' or a 'must' as we cannot predict how children will interpret the resources that they are given.

Under 'A', I would encourage you to list the possible outcomes an adult might achieve linked to your objectives and the resources. This is also a 'might' not a 'must' as an adult may go to work with some children in the sand and observe them doing something brilliant that is nothing to do with the objectives. What you don't want to happen is that an adult kills an interest or stops some brilliant play, just to get their objective in!

Planning for challenge in continuous provision

We should all be on a constant quest to ensure that quality learning is taking place for *all* our children. This can seem hard to do in continuous provision, which, although packed with potential, is also packed with unlimited opportunities for children to stagnate in low-level activities that challenge no one. One excellent method to help with this is to carry out an engagement/attainment audit.

Engagement/attainment audit

Pick a child and track them when they go into continuous provision. Every five minutes find them and write down exactly what they are doing. After an hour or so have a look at your list and then try to attach attainment for that child to the activity they were taking part in. Ask yourself:

- **Can I see engagement?** – You would hope that the answer to this question would be 'yes'. If children are not engaged that might indicate that there is an issue with your provision, so consider: is the provision linked to assessment? Is it appropriately levelled and dressed for interest?

- **Can I see attainment?** – Most importantly, can you attach attainment to what you are seeing, or are children happily engaged in low-level experience and learning?

Obviously attainment can be a subjective thing. It relies on the person observing having a good knowledge of the development of the children that you are looking at. I did an engagement/attainment audit in a Reception class alongside a headteacher, and we watched the play and learning within continuous provision with great interest. We were particularly interested in two boys outside who had taken a bucket of water and a sponge each from the 'car wash' and were sitting on a wall talking to each other while squeezing the sponge in the bucket. This went on for some considerable time. Just two boys, squeezing a sponge! As instructed, the headteacher asked herself the first key question: 'Can I see engagement?' Well, the answer to that was a definite 'yes' – the boys were very engaged in their sponge squeezing! Then she asked the second key question: 'Can I see attainment?' and decided that the answer to that question was 'no'. The boys had sat in the same spot for close to 20 minutes talking and giggling and doing a very good impression of messing about!

When the headteacher talked to the Early Years co-ordinator afterwards, she asked her if she had been correct in her judgement and if so, why had no one intervened and taken the play forward? The co-ordinator said that she too had spotted the 'sponge squeezers', one of whom had English as an additional language and as a result was a very reluctant speaker who often played alone or with an adult. The fact that he was engaged in an interaction with another child (and enjoying it) was a significant step for him, therefore she had left them to their sponge squeezing! That is why any observation or judgement should always have some context from the people who know the children best.

If you do observe your children and notice that a pattern of high-level engagement but low-level attainment repeats itself a number of times for several children then you have got a problem on your hands, especially if the children are compliant. Some will be happy to sit in your snack, mark making or construction area for 30 or 40 minutes getting on quietly, but producing something that they could have done this time last term or last year. Partly this will be because children like to make self-affirming, familiar choices and partly because the provision has not been set up for skill development, so even if an adult did intervene and try to promote more effective learning, the planning and resources are not in place to make that a very easy task.

If we have not identified key skills in our areas of provision, we are likely to have put out low-level familiar resources that just invite children to engage (happily) in low-level tasks. What you risk by not setting up the provision for skill development is long-term learning stagnation, where children become accustomed to lack of challenge. This can encourage children to 'butterfly' and visit lots and lots of different areas and activities because they are bored with the provision that you have put out. It can also result in children demonstrating inappropriate behaviours or just heading for the door as soon as it is opened and spending their entire time whizzing around on a scooter! There are a few key areas of continuous provision in which this 'stagnation' seems to occur more frequently, and they are: sand, water, malleable materials, workshop and paint.

So, how do we avoid the inevitable? Well, if you want to guarantee success and avoid stagnation in all areas of your environment, then you need to apply a multi-layered approach. If any of the layers are missing, you risk low-level learning and stagnation.

Implicit and explicit challenge

In any good Year One learning environment you should be able see evidence of both implicit and explicit challenge. Your continuous provision spaces should still look like a play space and feel like a play space to the children, but what I am talking about is the level of 'unseen' rigour that underpins it, put in place by us as well as the very obvious and direct, 'Can you do this?' challenges.

Implicit challenge

Implicit challenge involves:

- Creating an environment that is built on assessment, observation, next steps and children's interests.
- Striving to promote process rather than just outcome.

- Considering what your expectations are of children when they are playing in the spaces that you have created.

- Considering how what you have given the children will motivate, interest and inspire them to continue to learn in the absence of an adult.

- Levelling the common play behaviours to acknowledge a range of skills that children 'could' develop within an area of provision and then think about those skills as emergent, developing and high level.

- Thinking of each skill in that way will guide you to the type of resources that you want to make available to children in that area as continuous provision.

- Adding enhancements to this provision that could be linked to the theme you are discussing, children's interests, basic skills or area of learning, a specific skill or an explicit challenge.

Explicit challenge

Explicit challenges are easier than implicit ones – primarily because you are not 'implying' anything, you are asking the children, 'Can you do this?', often with the expectation that it isn't a choice!

If you find that you are giving children explicit challenges and they are not choosing to do them, then that probably says more about the challenges themselves than the children. The mantra that we need to keep in our head is that high-level engagement gives you the potential for high-level attainment. If they are not engaged, then they won't learn. A dull area of provision or a dull challenge will not produce a motivated learner.

Challenges linked to process not outcome

Although you might choose to include direct challenges as an element of your environment, what you need to be very careful of are challenges that are linked to outcome and not process. For example, in my painting area I might put a label over my easel that says, 'Can you paint a rocket?'. This is not an appropriate direct challenge – it doesn't matter what the children paint when they are working at the easel; it is how they paint and what they paint with that are the important bits.

If you were talking about space, or a group of children had a particular interest in rockets, then you might add an enhancement to the painting area in the form of a stimulus like a picture or a model. But there would be no expectation that everyone would paint one as lots of children are not interested in rockets and if that was their only option, they just wouldn't go near the easels.

A good example of challenge linked to process would be if you wanted the children to do some problem solving through play, you enhanced your continuous provision for sand with a bowl of lentils, a bowl of dried peas and a bowl of dry pasta. Alongside the continuous provision that you have already put in place for sieving and sifting, you might also add some extra enhancements. Your challenge might be: 'Could you mix the lentils, peas and pasta into the sand (giving it a good stir). Then, could you separate the lentils, peas and pasta again?'. This is a direct challenge that encourages process and application of prior knowledge rather than just a predetermined outcome.

As practitioners who promote learning through play, we also have to acknowledge that just because we added lentils, peas and pasta to our sand and gave the explicit challenge that children won't all use the resources in the way that we were intending. That is okay, because we want children to be able to interpret the environments that we create in a way that is meaningful to them and that is often in a way that we didn't think of or couldn't imagine.

6 An EYFS environment in Year One

In an ideal world, your Year One environment would be a lovely, light, open space with a variety of easy-to-access furniture and continuous provision for outdoor learning. Unfortunately, very few Year One classrooms can boast such a space. This is another added complication in trying to deliver an EYFS approach that your children will be used to in a space that isn't set up to support you. In truth, you can only work with what you have got in terms of space and furniture while continually re-evaluating your success and stumbling blocks in an effort to help you plan a better space. But, the EYFS ethos is not just about tables and chairs.

Display

Our children spend a great deal of time in their learning environment, so we need it to be meaningful to them. There is a huge amount of precious wall space at our disposal to fill with things that are going to inspire, teach and promote self-esteem. In that respect, our wall space should be a blank canvas that belongs to each new group of Year One children who come through the door. Children are unlikely to really engage with their space if it is full of someone else's work or an impersonal, downloaded, laminated display.

That is why, for the beginning of Year One, I would suggest that your walls are *blank*. They can be backed and bordered, but otherwise they are empty. True blank canvasses for the children to fill. I appreciate that for some people, the thought of doing this would be a huge leap of faith, but trust me, it is worth it in the long run. If you have display that is already up when the children come in to your setting then they will all notice it, but only a small number will really see it, and of that small number very few if any will go on seeing it and then using it to support their learning. It is not that it is magic display that can disappear, or that the children go blind! It just becomes very familiar and because they were not part of creating it and it isn't relevant to their learning, they just don't engage with it.

I know a lot of you may have seen your EYFS colleagues go through something of a display transformation where they no longer raid the art stock cupboard for the biggest and brightest backing paper and borders. Instead, they have begun to embrace their inner 'beige' – backing their boards in hessian and replacing their plastic boxes with wicker baskets.

This is not about some membership to an Early Years club, or that they are just jumping on the latest bandwagon. It is an approach based on making the environment as decodable and as motivational as possible for children. The ethos being that a neutral environment makes it easy for children to see the important things that we want them to notice and be motivated by seeing themselves and their work in action.

So, if we are going to strip all our boards and back them in preparation for our new cohort, what should these boards look like? In my day, I was the king of the contrasting backing and border. There was no combination too bold for me to try. Every board had a different coloured backing paper and often a number of colours in the border. I have backed in wrapping paper, foil, newsprint, wallpaper, print and collage. I have bordered with fairy lights, tinsel, leopard print, sweets and every mass-produced border roll there was going. Once I had finished, my classroom had the resemblance of a cross between Santa's grotto and a cheap brothel!

When you have really gone to town on a display, it is true that children will be excited by it because it has made your classroom look different. But after a while they will stop noticing it, as it is meaningless to them. As a Year One teacher, I once did a six-week topic on circus. I think I may have chosen it in the first place because of it's display potential! I got all of my children to lie on the floor and assume circus poses for me to draw round, like fire-eater and trapeze artist. We then spent (literally) weeks collaging, colouring and painting our characters – with a lot of assistance from the adults. After attaching a years' worth of crêpe paper to the ceiling to look like a tent and sticking my figures up around the room, I was done! The adults loved it – but in terms of impact on the childrens' learning, purpose and engagement, the whole thing was very questionable. If a child in your class has produced a brilliant piece of mark making and you have backed it in pink and orange and stuck it on a gold foil board with a glitter border, they will cease to see it because it will be lost amongst the brightness and the bling.

I often talk to Early Years practitioners about their walls being like an enlarged version of the learning journeys that they make for the children. A good display gives anyone looking at it a sense of the sort of learning opportunities that you provide for the children, how you have reflected and supported their interest, taught them skills, recorded their voice and shared your thoughts as a practitioner. This should be exactly the same ethos for Year One. If we fill our walls with too much computer-generated, laminated labelling, then we lose any individuality and specific meaning. Although we might feel like we have filled a space with something useful, uniform and attractive, we have to ask ourselves what tangible impact it is having on our children's learning – if any.

It is essential for children to be able to identify their own work within a display. This visual stimulus will remind their brain of what it was they were doing when they created that piece of work. It will also build on their sense of achievement and self-worth – how proud they were when you put it on the wall. This will then inspire them to apply the knowledge or skill that they used to other tasks that they do. Hence your display is having a direct impact on attainment.

But, they need to be able to see their work, hence the big push over the past few years for Early Years settings to embrace their love of hessian and all things neutral. Bland is good when it comes to backgrounds, because bland behind allows the children's work to stand out, and that is how it should be. For that to happen, your display boards need to be neutral, I would go as far as to say beige!

A common problem for settings that try the 'neutral' approach is that they go from being bright and cheery to being beige and boring. I think the key phrase to remember here is 'less is more *not* less is morgue'. Your classroom should be an exciting place to play and learn and display should be a reflection of that. It's just that the energy and 'wow' should come from the content not the dressing.

Getting children involved in display

Getting your children involved in the production and creation of your classroom display can also be a really powerful tool. Once they have some ownership over how the display space is going to be used and they have a role in decisions about how it will be used – they have more engagement with the display itself.

A mechanism that is often used in Early Years is 'self display', where the children have a low board where they can display their own work. Sometimes this will be a space where they stick their work in a particular area to show that they have done something, and other times it is a display space with a theme or a focus. The children know that if they produce a piece of work that fits the theme or the focus, they can display it on the board. There are lots of opportunities for discussion with the children about what they might choose to display and how they might display it.

Asking the children to make labels or titles for displays that you have created together is another way of getting their input and engagement into the environment. For a child, seeing your label appear on the wall not only individualises the space, but also gives a really strong sense of inclusion, ownership and engagement.

Think about gender

One point that is worth considering when you have finished your display is how the environment you have created will impact on gender. Some boys' aversion to all things pink is not a conscious thought process but a deeply ingrained learned response to gender roles that have been passed onto them. Usually these are well established by the time a child is about two.

When you are thinking about your display, make sure that your backgrounds are neutral but also that they do not cater too much for the preferences of one particular group of children. The game that I like to play with settings is: 'If you had to give "it" a gender, what gender would you give it?' The 'it' can be any aspect of your environment or provision, but in this case we are talking about display. If the answer to your question is clearly 'male' or 'female', then your dressing is not neutral enough. This should always be the case unless you have specifically dressed an area or a resource around the interests of a particular group of children, as discussed in Chapter 6, p.63.

'Gender' is *not* the same as 'sex'. The World Health Organisation (2015) says that:

'Gender refers to the socially constructed characteristics of women and men – such as norms, roles and relationships of and between groups of women and men. It varies from society to society and can be changed.'

So, it is possible to give the spaces that we create a gender while not necessarily intending them to be for 'boys' or 'girls'.

One of the issues that often arises in teaching spaces is that because they are predominantly created by humans with a strong female gender imprint, they can then appear very feminine to children who have a more culturally-stereotypically masculine gender.

Gender stereotyping is a complex and subtle thing and most children have got a very strong gender imprint by the time that they are two. The socially-accepted view of the gender that has been attached to their biological state will have been thrust upon them from the moment they were born, from the colour of Babygro™ we put them in, to the type of language and cultural references that we use about and to them.

When we are thinking about the environments and displays that we create in school, and how they appear to all children, then all of that gender stereotyping and conformity comes into play – not all of the time with every child, but most of the time with most children.

Print-rich or just full of print?

'Print-rich' is a lovely phrase, but it is one that is easily misinterpreted and can cause practitioners a great deal of angst, not to mention headaches for children! So, what is a print-rich environment? Well, for me the most important word in the phrase is not 'print', it is 'rich'. If we think about the word rich in monetary terms, it just means that you have got a lot of it. But when it comes to learning through print, less is often more – at least to start with.

Print in your environment is only rich for children if they are interested in it and engage with it. If there is lots of it, then it just becomes wallpaper. At the early stages of development, when children are recognising different letter and number shapes, print doesn't only just need to be engaging, it needs to be clear. To an 'emerging eye', the printed letters a, o, b, d, c, p, q, e and g can look very similar, so if they are displayed all in the same font and colour within a very busy background then chances are they won't be as engaging. If we use print in the environment to teach children that print carries meaning, then it makes sense for children to be involved in the creation of that print. This could be labels for the classroom or for a display.

Recording on a display what the children say about their work, or what they think about what they have been doing, along with their photograph can be a great way of getting them to engage with the print that is on the walls. I would say that there also needs to be a variety of styles of print mixed in, with adults' and children's mark making and writing that has been done 'live' in the setting. The main body of print on your walls should be meaningful and relevant to the children and produced by an adult or child working in the space. Then enhancements to your printed environment can be made using other examples and styles of print. But you should view this sort of print in the same way as you do an enhancement to any part of your provision, as just that – an enhancement.

It can be a really good idea to have labels near to particular provisions to help, support and focus children's learning, but only if the children actually engage with the print. A good idea is to use the children themselves to make the labels. Then you can talk about ideas and expectations while you are making them and the children will have a memory prompt when they look at them. If in doubt, do the squint test. Stand about six feet away from your display board and squint at it. If the children's work, the background, the border and the labelling all merge into one riot of colour and pattern then you have got it wrong. If the children's work pings out at you (and them), then you have got it right. After all, what is display for? It is there to motivate children by raising their self-esteem or to teach them something that they need to know. It is not about making wallpaper. There will be lots and lots of other opportunities for you to introduce print into your environment through books, comics, letters, etc. First make sure your walls are print-rich and not just full of print.

Display content

A good display can have many purposes, but they should all be linked to learning in some way, shape or form. For me, display tends to fall into three broad categories:

- teach and inspire
- celebrate
- document.

I would list them in that order of importance and prominence within your environment.

If I said that I would start by linking your display to assessment, it all begins to sound a little bit (well, a lot) dry and dull. But, the use of assessment and observation is crucial when you are planning next steps for children and if you want your display to show learning and differentiation, then it needs to be linked to your assessments. We don't often think about a display being able to teach, but really that should be one of their primary functions. But to teach successfully you need to engage, and that can be where some displays fall down.

To engage you have to be visible. I am not going to interact with something that I can't see or access. So, the ideal height for your teaching display is child's eye level. As human beings we look ahead and down most of the time. This is how nature made us, so that we could scan the horizon for predators and prey and also look for food, resources (and big holes that we might fall into and die) on the ground. We had very few predators from above and few resources and food sources, therefore we don't really look up unless prompted to do so.

The further up the wall your display is, the less impact it will have from children without direction to it. This also applies when we are hanging copious amounts of 'stuff' from the ceiling, on hoops, washing lines and bits of string! Ask yourself who looks at it? Who is it for? Is is for children? Also, what impact does it have on teaching and learning, and how does it impact on cluttering my space?

How many children ever approached a water tray and said, 'Now, before we start engaging in water play, let's just cast our eyes in a heavenly direction and reflect on some of these appropriately-placed adjectives that link to water play'? The answer is none – *ever*! Does it really make it a print-rich space, when the drops are all the same size and same colour and printed in the same font and twirling round in the breeze? No! So, what is it for? Even though I have created many versions of this sort of display in my time for 'children', the answer is that this sort of display is for adults, because we like it, it looks co-ordinated and attractive and we can make the link between adjectives and learning. But children just don't.

As adults our brains are really good at taking in a lot of information and being able to sort it and process it quickly and efficiently. For the majority of children, they have not developed that skill to such a high level when they are in Year One. So, when they walk into a busy space, they don't see it in the same way that we do. Their visual discrimination isn't as well-honed as ours so everything tends just to become background wallpaper. It is not that they have a visual impairment or the walls go all wobbly and blurry like on Scooby Doo! But everything tends just to become background wallpaper.

I know that most Year One classrooms have not been built with this concept in mind. Often children's eye level is full of cupboards, sinks, trunking, units, tables etc., which is not ideal, but you can only work with what you have got and sometimes you have to get a bit creative, re-positioning your furniture and using the backs of units for display. I know this will sound like an April fool, but seriously, it is worth getting down onto your knees and walking around your space. It will give you a really good child's eye view of what you have got to work with. It can be equally as productive to do your outdoor space as well, but get some knee pads or kneel on a skateboard and get someone else to push you round – now that is how you put the fun back into team meetings!

Once you have got your eye level sorted out, this is where you are going to put your key teaching display. Things like phonic lines, alphabet charts, number lines etc. – all of the things that you want the children to engage with and use. Next step is to ask yourself what are young children motivated by more than anything else? More than their favourite television character? And more than sweets? THEMSELVES! They are ego mad. They love nothing better than to see themselves on a video or in a photo. So if we are trying to create a display that will really motivate and engage them in their learning – a display that they want to interact with and return to – what should we use in that display? You got it – THEM!

There are all sorts of ways that you can use children's images in display and, bearing in mind that you have just stripped all of your walls, we had better get started at exploring some possibilities. The more you can personalise your display to your current cohort, the more likely they are to engage with it, so consider using children's images to create any number lines, alphabet or phonic prompts, reminders of rules and routines as well as instructions for game play or activities. One way of doing this would be to create a learning wall.

Learning wall

In EYFS the children will probably have had some sort of learning journey or journal. This is a document that celebrates and tracks the unique and individual progress of that child's learning during their time in EYFS. A sign of a good learning journey is one that is unique to the child. If every child has got the same sort of activity stuck on the same page on the same date, then it is not so much a learning journey as a diary of activities.

Some settings in Year One (and beyond) continue with the idea of the learning journey – carrying on with examples of children's work. It can be really effective on entry to Year One to think of your display as a learning journey, just on the wall rather than in a book or folder. You use your display to show how you followed children's interests as well as themes that you introduced to them. You can show attainment, differentiation, adult thinking and children's voice, and fill your display board with all of the great stuff that you are doing.

This not only serves as a great self-esteem builder for the children, but also as an effective learning wall to share with parents and staff, making the more subtle aspects of play-based learning easier to interpret.

The criteria for children for getting their work onto the wall can range from it being something that they are proud of and want to display to something that they have done really well and an adult wants to feature. What is in the space will change over time but regularly it changes is up to you. Here are some fundamental concepts that are worth considering with this type of display:

- The children's work is the feature, so it shouldn't have to compete with the background.

- Try and give it some relevance by including some direct speech from the child.

- Try adding your thoughts as a practitioner, outlining some of the context around the activity.

- If you are working in line with the principles of EYFS to support transition, consider adding some next steps statements. This not only helps to clarify the thinking of the team but also makes it much easier to judge attainment and be aware of how learning happens in Early Years, especially if you are not an Early Years expert.

7 Learning and teaching in Year One

So far I have discussed lots of the 'mechanics' that go into building a successful play-based approach to learning in Year One. But, once you have used your GSA to create your areas of provision, then your common play behaviours to help you to resource your continuous provision and sorted out your enhancements and your explicit challenges – how do you actually make it all work? For me, the secret to a successful learning space comes in how the adult facilitates learning. This is a play-based approach, so we are supporting the children's learning through play. We are not just saying, 'Off you go, I will call you over when it is your turn to read.'

All of the structure that you have put in place in your environment can be very quickly undone if there is not an adult in the play with the children to facilitate their learning. We need to be in the play with them so that we can observe, support, challenge, scaffold as well as manage and reset the provision.

That is all well and good, but if you are up to your elbows in sand, when does the maths get taught? The answer for me is that it gets taught while you are up to your elbows in the sand! I am going to go on to talk about an example timetable that has worked very effectively in Year One (and Reception). Key to this timetable being really successful is two mechanisms that you might want to consider:

- staggered entry to continuous provision
- objective-led planning.

Staggered entry to continuous provision

There are many variations to a staggered entry to provision and they usually depend on the size and layout of your space and the number of adults that you have got working in Year One. The basic principle is that you would gather your children together for some sort of direct input. This could be as a whole class or they might be in groups. If you are delivering to your whole class, then everyone would get the same input, with some differentiated questioning and explanation. Then, when you felt that your less mature/lower ability children had reached their capacity for attention and learning, they would leave the group and go into provision. This could be a time of free choice or you may consider giving them an explicit challenge to complete before moving into free choice.

You would extend your input to the rest of your group a little further, then your next group would go into the provision – maybe five minutes later. You would further extend your input with the remaining children, then they and you would join everyone in the provision. That way, each group has the input and follow-up that is suitable to their level of understanding.

If you have got more adults to work with the children, then they could either take a group for the input and then go into provision with their group when they have finished or, if you were delivering a whole class session, they could support you with the whole group while you were giving the carpet input and then go into provision with the first group to leave.

Using your continuous provision planning

Once the children are in provision, adults need to avoid the temptation to sit behind a table and call groups to work with them. This is primarily for two reasons: first, you don't get the same level of engagement from the children, and second, if you aren't in the provision you are going to miss lots of opportunities for learning and support.

As I have said, the role of the adult in provision can be a diverse one. You are there to observe, support, challenge and scaffold as well as manage and reset the area. Often you will see children producing some brilliant self-initiated learning using the resources that you have provided that is not necessarily anything to do with the plan that you had in your head. You will also get lots of opportunities to deliver what you need to 'teach' while supporting the children's play. Your 'taught' adult input will come from your continuous provision planning (see Chapter 5, p.55) and any enhancement that you have added that is linked to an adult focus or an objective-led plan (see below).

Do you remember the example plan for continuous provision in Chapter 5 (p.56)? In the planning, the teacher recorded what an adult 'might' do with the enhancements they had put into their provision. So, you and your adults know how they can use enhancements to help you to support learning gaps you have identified. I don't want to sound like I am nagging, but it is really important to remember that it is a 'might' and not a 'must'. We need to carefully assess what it is we are looking at when children are working in these areas before we steam in with a question!

Objective-led planning

The other mechanism you can use to make your timetable really effective is called objective-led planning. I really enjoy working with objective-led planning because it not only supports you in covering all of the teaching that your assessment is telling you that you need to do, it also allows you to work alongside the children in their space where their motivation is highest. For me, I like it because I get the chance to 'teach' rather than to 'deliver'. Because all of the children are not sitting in front of me in pre-determined ability groups taking part in an activity that I have planned, I have to use my ingenuity to assess their understanding and make my teaching points without feeling like I am crowbarring it in.

First you decide on which aspect of a subject you are going to focus on. It could be calculations, talk, upper body movement, pencil grip, ability to independently access the painting area – anything that has been identified by assessment, observation or curriculum coverage as a need. You group your children by their ability within this aspect. Then, on your planning sheet, you make a statement of *current* attainment under each group of children. So, in your chosen focus you make a note of where they are now on transition to Year One. For some children this statement will come from *Early Years Outcomes* and for others it may come from the National Curriculum. This is an important stage in the planning process because it crystallises your thoughts about what you think these children are capable of and how you know it. It also lets the whole team know what you are thinking.

Then you make a 'next steps' statement of attainment for each group. This can be tricky, especially if you are not really familiar with *Early Years Outcomes* but it's really just the same principle as differentiating the activity for your groups if you had been calling them out to work with you. It is these next step that you then take into the children's play. I would *not* call groups of children to me; the success of objective-led planning is based on the fact that you go to them. When you go and play alongside children, you get high levels of engagement. If you come across a group of children of mixed ability – which you will, because children don't tend to play in ability groups! – you just differentiate your questioning to suit the next steps objectives for the ability group of the child you are working with.

If I know that I have got a group of children who have a particular interest in something like cars, dinosaurs, princesses or spiders then I might create a provocation or 'starter activity' that I know is going to grab their interest (see p.75). Once they have visited my activity and I have fulfilled my teaching objective, then I wouldn't start calling other children over. The activity has fulfilled its purpose in attracting the children that I was targeting. I would now take my objectives into other children's play.

When the children are in continuous provision, the adults will go into that play not only to look for opportunities for assessment and observation, and to support children's play and discovery but also to teach. The adults deliver an objective that had been identified by assessment as a need that has then been broken down into next steps for each ability group. This objective-led planning might be linked to the direct teaching sessions, or it might be linked to any other aspect of the EYFS or National Curriculum that your assessment and observation has identified as a need.

This planning for adults in continuous provision would probably last for a week. I say 'probably' because children are not an exact science and sometimes an objective will take much longer to cover than others. During that week the adult (or adults) responsible for that objective would try to deliver it to all of the children at least once through play. They would probably not have a planned activity that they took around the setting. Instead they would look for opportunities to deliver the next steps objectives through what was engaging the children the most. If a child you were working with didn't understand or achieve the objective, you could revisit it a number of times in a number of different areas across the week. By the same token, if a child clearly showed that they were beyond the objective that you had set for them, you could revise that objective and deliver it to them again in a different play situation.

The most important part of objective-led planning to reiterate is that you take your planning into play to deliver the appropriate objectives to the appropriate children. I know I have mentioned this before, but it is a really important point that is worth stressing again. Plus, it is the aspect of objective-led planning that most practitioners struggle with.

The whole concept is that an objective-led plan is *one* mechanism used by adults to support children's learning in your Year One continuous provision environment. Because our environment has been linked to assessment, implicitly levelled and enhanced with specific resources, it is a quality learning environment that will offer lots of valuable and useful learning opportunities that aren't linked to one specific objective. Adults will also observe, support, challenge and teach around concepts and skills that arise through children's interaction with the space that are nothing to do with the objective recorded on their plan. Therefore when an adult has an objective-led plan – unlike an activity list – the idea is not that you work through the children as fast as possible until you have got through everyone on your list.

I appreciate that it can be hard if you have never done it before, but you need to get into the habit of unpicking what you see while the children are playing and deciding whether you need to leave them alone and move on. Observe and record what they are doing, join them and offer some sort of support or scaffolding to the learning that is taking place or, if appropriate, deliver your objective.

I have found that any more than three objective-led planning sheets in any one setting become hard to manage and track. In larger settings, adults often double up on one objective and just present it in different ways.

Here is an example of an objective-led planning sheet:

Focus:	Next Steps:	Evidence/Activity starter:
Group one	**Next steps for this group**	
Statement of current attainment		
Group two	**Next steps for this group**	
Statement of current attainment		
Group three	**Next steps for this group**	
Statement of current attainment		
Group four	**Next steps for this group**	
Statement of current attainment		
EYFS links:		

Figure 8: *Objective-led planning sheet example.*

Starter activities/provocations

In an ideal world, I would use objective-led planning all of the time for the periods of the school day that are continuous provision, but I appreciate that initially some adults won't be comfortable with this kind of teaching. In that case, what you might want to consider doing is having some sort of provocation or starter activity that has been set up by the adult. This could be linked to the topic or theme that you are talking about or the interests of a specific group of children. You would set it up and make it clear to the children that this is where you were starting the session.

The important thing to remember is that you are using the provocation or starter activity as a springboard, something to get you started. When the interest in your starter activity begins to dwindle, you are not going to go out on the prowl with your list of children who haven't done it yet, and drag them in! You would leave your activity and go into the provision with your objectives, looking for opportunities to deliver your next steps. Regardless of how good you are or how exciting your activity seems to you, there will be children who are far more motivated by doing other things. You need to seek out their area of motivation and capitalise on it.

How it can work with and without a starter activity

One setting that I was working in were trialing working with and without a starter activity. This was partly just to see what difference it made and also because one member of staff felt more confident with a starting point rather than heading off into continuous provision armed with nothing more than a clipboard – if you are used to being given an activity planner and a group of children to work with, then this can be a very scary prospect.

In the following example, in the classroom there is a teacher and a teaching assistant (TA). The teacher is working without a starter activity; the TA is working with a starter activity.

The teacher:

- has a writing focus for her objective-led planning
- is going to get the children to write using their knowledge of phonics
- has grouped all of the children by their phonic knowledge and given each group a 'next steps' statement
- has *not* planned an activity.

The teacher moved from area to area, observing children, supporting their learning and also delivering her objectives. She found opportunities for mark making and writing in all areas.

The TA:

- has a talk focus for her objective-led planning
- is working on the children using talk for instructions
- also wants to combine her objective-led planning with teaching the children how to use a toaster, as Year One have decided they are going to have a rolling snack, funded by the parents.

The TA starts in the new snack area with the toaster. As this activity not only involves food but specifically toast, she doesn't have to ask twice for volunteers!

The adult is modelling the process of making toast using the language that has been planned for her on her objective-led plan. The children are talking about what she is doing. She then lets them have a turn at toasting a slice of bread, following the agreed rules for safety and also using the language of instruction. After approximately ten minutes, the TA puts the toaster away and moves out of the snack area. The children can still access the snack area, there is just no provision for making toast.

The adult moves through the space looking for opportunities to deliver her objective. After approximately 30 minutes she returns to the snack area, gets out the toaster and begins the process with another group of children. Again after a short period of time, the toaster goes away and the adult moves into the continuous provision. She will carry on doing this until all of the children have experienced the learning objective.

Timetabling

When it comes to timetabling, there needs to be a good balance between adult-led and child-initiated teaching and learning. Although no two schools have exactly the same timetable, there are similarities that exist in most. In the current climate, I tend to find that there is a very strong leaning towards adult-led delivery. This is because this style of teaching puts the adult very much in control and makes tracking input and evidence very easy, although it is not always the best model for learning.

There will be some direct teaching in Year One, especially with regard to children's acquisition of the basic skills of literacy and numeracy. Having said that, there has to be a balance. As Year One teachers, we need to acknowledge what is *appropriate* for the stage of development of our children and should keep that firmly in mind if we are being asked to jump onto the latest literacy or numeracy bandwagon that will have our children sitting on the carpet 'chanting' for ridiculously long periods of time.

Assessment is the most important tool that we have got at our disposal for letting us know what to teach and when to teach it. If children are not ready for a particular stage of learning, then we should be using our resources to help to prepare them. If they are more than ready, then we should take them to the next step on their learning journey.

There is no such thing as the 'perfect timetable'. Timetables will change as the needs of the children change. In lots of larger settings you do not have the luxury of complete freedom with your timetables as there are so many other restrictions that are imposed upon you over which you have no control (assembly or ICT time, for example). Everyone's timetable will be different and you have to do the best with what you have got.

After working with a number of settings over many years to support them in implementing objective-led planning within the restrictions of their timetable, the following is the generic template that I have come up with. It has had to be 'tweaked' by each individual setting that has used it, but it might give you a starting point to get you going.

Obviously, at the beginning of the year, or for a new intake, it would be very different as children are getting used to you and your setting. Ultimately what we are aiming for is a timetable with a lot of fluidity and the minimum number of breaks. But, at the beginning of the year, you undoubtedly have a timetable that reflects the opposite. You would be doing lots of stopping and starting to help children to be clear about how to use your space appropriately, with lots of very public displays of delight when they achieve it.

Timetable template

At the point you are introducing this sort of timetable, you will have already:

- structured your environment around needs identified by your last summative assessment and ongoing observations.
- levelled your continuous provision in each area linked to assessment.
- dressed some of your continuous provision for interest.
- created opportunities for exploration, problem solving and thinking.

Within this timetable there are going to be opportunities for:

- direct teaching.
- teaching through continuous provision using objective-led planning.
- observing, assessing and supporting children's learning.
- finding time to talk to children and find out what interests and motivates them.

Time of the day	Provision overview
START OF THE DAY	• Self-registration • Linked provision • All together interest session • Dough gym/funky fingers time • Direct teach session 1 • Continuous provision session 1 • Brief tidy-up • Direct teach session 2 • Assess and review session
LUNCHTIME	• Toilet, hand wash, lunch
AFTERNOON	• Afternoon registration • Assess and review session • Direct teach 3 • Continuous provision session 2 • Tidy-up time • Carpet session

Figure 9: *Timetable template overview.*

Overview

You will notice three things missing from the template in Figure 9: playtimes, snacks and PE. These are discussed on p.86, after I have explained the different sessions on the timetable.

Self-registration

I would recommend that you start your day with self-registration, where children can use a variety of methods to show that they are present such as posting their name in a letterbox or using an interactive whiteboard registration programme. It is much quicker and far more empowering than 'Everyone sit on the carpet and say "hello" in a circle'. It is used really effectively throughout EYFS, so there is definitely no excuse in Year One!

The reason that I like it so much is not just because it helps to develop children's independence and self-reliance, but because it also frees up adults to interact and support learning rather than go through the ineffective and over-rehearsed routines of days of the week and the weather.

During long periods of registering time on the carpet, I always think about my attainment audit. What is the potential for progress or attainment when we ask children to sit for long periods of time and listen to us? Surely there would be more opportunities for engagement and learning if they were self-registering and then getting stuck into their learning?

Linked provision

This is that *short* session of provision that was discussed in Chapter 4, p.52. It takes place while the children are arriving and self-registering. It didn't exist in my first versions of this timetable but was introduced in response to a need identified mainly by Reception teachers in schools. The continuous provision here is not throughout the whole space but is usually just on a table. It is a game or play-based and can be linked to an area of development identified by assessment.

Practitioners will often base their linked provision on something that they have had a focus on the week before. It enables them to see whether their children have taken on board the learning and can demonstrate their new found skills in independent work. When this is the case, I would plan a weekly focus and have the same activities out every day for that week.

This session has also been used very successfully as a time to hear readers. Rather than pulling children out of learning during their longer continuous provision sessions, this session is used every day for an adult to hear individual or guided reading. Depending on the number of adults that you have got available and the length of the session, will dictate the number of readers that you can hear. As the same provision is going to be available at this time all week then children are not as likely to 'miss an opportunity' if they are asked to go and read.

Adult role

This session can only work if there are a minimum of two adults. One adult will welcome the children and facilitate the self-registration and access to the linked provision. The other adult will be doing some direct input such as hearing readers or speech and language intervention.

All together interest session

This is a daily session in which everyone comes together on the carpet to talk. During this session children will have the opportunity to discuss the things that are important to them. Adults will be able to introduce ideas and concepts to children and signpost learning opportunities that are available that day.

It is from this session that you will record children's interests and then use that information to shape your planning and provision. It is also a great time to do a bit of assessing and reviewing. I would recommend always have a weekly focus for this talk session, based on the type of talk that assessment had identified that the children needed to develop. Record this talk focus on your weekly planning and also indicate any key vocabulary that you feel the children need to develop in relation to it. This way you are showing how you are using assessment to identify need and then how you are planning to meet that need.

Adult role

If there are two adults, then one will lead the session while the other resets the environment after the linked provision session ready for the next session. As this is not a taught session then it is a legitimate use of the other adult's time to set up the provision for the next session. They can join the discussion as soon as the set up is complete.

Dough gym/funky fingers time

Every day the children need to engage in some sort of intervention that is going to help them to develop their gross and fine motor skills as well as their sense of balance, co-ordination and proprioception. Even your more dexterous children in Year One will benefit from this sort of intervention for five minutes each day. It is great for getting their blood pumping and their brains working at the beginning of the day. You can run dough gym and funky fingers at the same time so that all children are having a daily intervention that is supporting and extending their gross and fine motor development.

First of all, you will need to assess where the children are currently in terms of their dexterity and then identify what the next steps are. To do this you need to take into account a child's grip with a variety of objects of different sizes and also their ability to use their own fingers, or manipulate apparatus or resources to pick up small objects. Then you can use this information to create activities that will challenge and extend the children.

Dough gym

The children who need more gross motor development can work with an adult on an initiative like dough gym. Dough gym is a gym for children where you work out with dough to music. I have found that music is key to its success. Children are highly engaged by music and the beat is crucial when it comes to performing the dough gym moves. Choose

your music carefully – something that is popular and current is far more likely to get high levels of engagement than working out to 'Jesus' hands were kind hands'!

I work with at most eight children, not a whole group, and I make sure the children who need this intervention feel special and chosen for all of the right reasons, not just because they are failing. This initiative is about targeting specific areas of development; it has to be regular and consistent if it is going to have impact. As you want dough gym to carry a bit of prestige and have the 'envy factor', it is better if it is done in your main space and that children aren't taken off to the 'sunshine room' to do it!

This is how it works:

- The children present you with their dough gym membership cards and then take up their places.
- It is important that the children stand, as part of this initiative is to develop their balance, posture, proprioception, hand-eye co-ordination and bi-lateral movement, which is less effective when you sit down.

- Children's backs need to be straight and their legs shoulder-width apart. The children will find it very tempting to bend forward thus using their back rather than their shoulders and arms to support the dough. I always tell mine to squeeze their bum cheeks as this tightens the core and helps prevent bending.

- When the music starts, begin with shoulder pivots and arm stretches utilising the biggest range of movement interspersed with wrist, hand and finger exercises.

- Use the dough for resistance work. Anything from squashing it with a flat palm and a straight arm to pinching small bits out of it. The large ball of dough is also useful for developing arm muscles and pivots by lifting, as well as hand arches and finger pivots by squeezing.

- The session should be fast paced and hard work but most of all fun. You want to keep those children coming back for more.

(*Getting Ready to Write*, Bryce-Clegg)

Adult role

The role of the dough gym leader is quite like that of a slightly crazed aerobics instructor. Once the children become familiar with a few basic moves then you will be able to sequence them just by calling out the name of the move when you want the children to change. As the children become more proficient, you add more moves and create a more complex and challenging workout.

Funky fingers time

With one group of children working with an adult having a dough gym session, the rest of the children will be split into groups identified by assessment of their need and stage of development. They will each have a task to complete, such as how many pompoms can they move from the pot to the eggbox with the tweezers? How fast can they fill the skewer with beads and then empty it again?

If you have two adults in the room, it is advisable to have no more than five groups in total (including dough gym):

1. dough gym
2. threading cheerios onto spaghetti
3. fastening and unfastening buttons
4. squeezing tennis balls
5. picking sequins off sticky-backed plastic.

Make sure everyone knows where their funky fingers group is and on your command they should take their places! The music goes on and everyone is working at the same time. You will be amazed how tiring funky fingers activities can be!

Use the same funky fingers activities for a week. The level of challenge can be increased for different groups by asking them to complete the task faster or more times in a given time frame. Sometimes you will get a group of children whose dexterity is amazing – they could pick up a speck of dust with one eye closed! For these children I usually organise some sort of activity that you can do to music that is linked to the principles of Brain Gym™. One setting I have worked with does a very effective aerobics class with lots of cross body, bi-lateral movements and a couple of maracas thrown in for good measure! (*Getting Ready to Write*, Bryce-Clegg)

Adult role

In this session, the adult is either leading a specific group or supervising a number of groups.

Direct teach session 1

This session usually lasts between 15 and 25 minutes depending on the age of the children and their stage of development. This is a daily session. Usually you will be planning for three of these (see timetable template overview in Figure 9). If you are working with a continuous provision model in Year One, then remember that we want to keep it as 'continuous' as possible. For that reason, your direct teaching sessions will be at the beginning and/or end of your sessions of continuous provision.

One of the key things about effective direct teaching in groups is that you can do it through other areas of learning. It is easy to get stuck in the rut of constantly delivering the direct teaching sessions on the carpet facing the whiteboard. But, if you have created areas of provision in your Year One classroom because they engage children, then it makes sense to use them in your teaching sessions.

Adult role

If there is more than one adult in your classroom then it is possible to take groups of children into other areas of provision where you cannot only deliver your teaching point but also demonstrate a skill or piece of equipment. Each adult's role is to deliver a planned objective to a designated group of children through other areas of the environment and other areas of learning.

If you have got different adults working in different areas of the environment then this allows different groups to have virtual base times of different lengths. If I had a group of children who were at the stage of needing more time to complete an extended piece of writing, then I could keep my virtual base group working for a little while longer while the others finished and moved into continuous provision.

If your other adults are not comfortable or able to take a group, then make sure they are supporting you directly during your teaching. Are they sitting with a designated group to give further questioning or support? They should definitely not be carrying out housekeeping duties or sitting on a chair at the side of the carpet while you are teaching.

Continuous provision session 1

The children leave their adult focus and the adults move with them into continuous provision. At this point the adults would pick up their objective-led planning focus, as they will be looking for opportunities to deliver that alongside observing, assessing and generally supporting the children's interests.

What adults must *not* do is to pick up their objective-led planning and approach it like a tick list, hunting children down! This planning had been put in place to support learning and provide extra focus for attainment, not to dominate learning at all costs.

You are going to run one more direct teaching session before lunch so this session of continuous provision should last until then.

Adult role

Your role here is to support children's learning and development both indoors and out, using the differentiated provision and objective-led planning.

Brief tidy-up

This is not a complete environment overhaul but a brief reset that will allow the following direct teach session to be effective.

Direct teach session 2

This is your second direct teach of the day (if appropriate). It should run under the same principles as before, just with a different teaching focus.

Assess and review

At the end of the direct teach session and just before lunch is a great opportunity to gather together and have a brief assess and review session where the children can have the opportunity to talk about what they have done.

Toilet, hand wash, lunch

Time for lunch and a lie down!

Afternoon registration

This can be a quick whip through the register or self-registration and then meet on the carpet.

Assess and review session

This is an opportunity to meet together on the carpet to talk about what the children have done so far today and signpost possible learning opportunities for the afternoon.

Direct teach session 3

This is your third and final direct teach of the day. It should run under the same principles as before just with a different teaching focus.

Continuous provision session 2

The children leave their direct teach and the adults move with them into continuous provision, picking up their objective-led planning focus as before.

Tidy-up time

This is your tidy-up at the end of the day. Hopefully this slot will get shorter, the better children get at tidying up!

Carpet session

I like a decent carpet session at the end of the day where you can pull everything together and swap some stories about how your day has been and then enjoy a good book and a song before the rush to get your coat. When you are building in timings to your timetable, try and make some decent provision for both talk and story at the end of the day.

Playtime, PE and snack time

Three things that don't feature in this timetable are playtime, snack time and PE. The reason for this is that we are trying to achieve constancy and flow in children's learning with as few breaks as possible, so as a result we need to look carefully at all of the aspects of our practice and provision that cause these learning breaks and then evaluate them for their impact on attainment.

Playtime and PE

If playtime and PE are regular features of your school's approach to Year One, then consider bringing them in slowly. Remember, at the beginning of the year you are trying to make your routines feel as much like EYFS as possible for best transition. In EYFS the children would have access to the outdoors so don't usually have a timetabled playtime. This means that their session of continuous provision can run for up to and over an hour. If you have access to an outdoor space in Year One, you might want to consider also not going out for playtime (especially early in the children's transition).

I appreciate that this isn't always easy, as the Year One staff may well be on the rota for playground duty or assembly cover. So, when you are working out your transition policy and practice, it is worth having the discussion about you joining the playtime rota when (and if) you begin to introduce it into your day.

Snack time

Many Year One settings carry on providing snacks for children. Like with every area of your provision, it is worth asking the question: 'What is snack time for in Year One?' before you start to plan for it.

You can view your snack time purely as a refuelling session – a space for hungry children to come and recharge their batteries with a bit of fruit or a slice of toast. But, in truth, there are so many other really effective reasons to maintain snack time in Year One.

There are many aspects of learning and social interaction that can be developed during snack time, but usually only if there is an adult there to facilitate them. Snack time is a great opportunity to develop language and social interaction, but if children have limited vocabulary and social skills, then they are not going to interact with each other. These skills will not develop on their own.

During their settling-in period in Reception, a collective snack time was probably used for reminding the children of appropriate behaviour, routines, celebrations of good work and behaviour, as well as what snack time is all about – how you eat your snack, how to pour your water, etc. If you feel that your children need that opportunity to stop and gather their thoughts on entry to your classroom then you could employ that strategy again. Although, I wouldn't keep it in place for too long as snack sessions are notorious for eating into your timetable if everyone stops and eats at the same time.

Another situation where you might consider a stop and sit down snack would be to help you to establish your relationship with the children. Food is a very social thing and meeting and eating in small groups can really help to develop relationships as well as provide fantastic opportunities for adults to tap into children's interests and then use what they have found out to link into learning for high-level engagement.

Usually as time goes on and the children get better at using the environment independently, you will do far less stopping and starting as you want to facilitate opportunities for deep-level learning, exploration and discovery. This is when a self-service snack comes into its own.

Children should have been very used to self-serving their snack in Reception so you don't need to have someone stationed at the snack table just in case someone should come along looking hungry. The role of the adult is too precious not to have them moving through the provision supporting children. Snacking like this is brilliant for supporting independence and interaction but as there is no adult 'manning' the space it can also become a haven for 'avoiders' who will happy sit and spend half an hour chewing on an apple.

Alongside the independence element of the snack area, you also want to introduce other learning opportunities. This can be as simple as having a photograph or object on the table for the children to look at and talk about.

For any continuous provision to be effective, adults need to be mobile within the learning space. You should be taking learning to children rather than pulling children to you. If you set up an activity at a table in one area of your setting and then call children to you, it becomes impossible for you to then ensure that what is going on in your continuous provision is really taking children's learning forward and not just low-level holding tasks. So, as an adult is moving through the learning space they are able to drop into the snack area, reset any of the resources that need resetting, check for loiterers and engage in a bit of quality talk. If you are trying to encourage children to talk then you need to give them something that they are going to want to talk about. Humour and terror (within reason) often work well, as does showing them photos of past events, getting them to remember, recall, sequence and articulate their memories.

There will also be times when you work in the snack area alongside the children to help them to prepare what they are going to eat and then join them in eating it!

Planning

If you use all of the timetabling, teaching and planning mechanisms that I have talked about in this book, on a weekly planner you would need to show your planning for:

- Direct teaching sessions – literacy, mathematics, phonics, or whatever else your direct teaching sessions were going to focus on. This planning should show differentiation and indicate which adults will be teaching which groups.

- Talk focus for interest discussions and carpet times – this just needs to record what type of talk you will be focusing on and any key vocabulary that you would like practitioners to use. This talk will be a predominant focus at carpet times, but if adults know what the focus is then they will be able to use it throughout the setting as and when it is appropriate.

- Self-registration and linked provision – if you are going to utilise the beginning of the day to target a specific area of learning in your linked provision, then you would need to record what that was and why you were doing it, referencing assessment data or whole school/setting initiatives.

- Dough gym/funky fingers activities – depending on how many groups you have for your five-minute physical intervention this could just be a simple activity list indicating any resources needed.

- Objective-led planning (for each session of continuous provision) – this is the planning that your adults will be taking with them to support teaching and learning in continuous provision. This planning needs to show which aspect you are going to be teaching, the children's current attainment in that aspect and their next steps targets. It is *really* important to remember that this is *not* a tick list and should be delivered in several areas of the environment through children's play.

- Continuous provision and enhancements – if you have identified areas that you feel are stagnating and you want to enhance them with a skills focus, then your planning needs to show which areas you are focusing on, the differentiation of the skill and any resourcing that you need to include to support development (see Chapter 5, p.55).

If all of the above is visible in your setting, it is not only a constant reminder for all practitioners, but it can also help anyone who is coming into your setting to assess progress and learning to know what to look for and also understand how attainment can work in Year One.

8 Effective transition: a case study

The introduction of the Foundation Stage framework made some significant differences to the way that children were taught in their nursery and Reception years. Not only did it have a large impact on what they were taught, it also radically changed the environment in which they were taught.

Previously, Reception and Year One environments had been very similar in most settings and the transition between the two year groups was relatively straight-forward. This positive change to our education system for children in the Early Years began to produce some negative outcomes when they moved into Key Stage One.

The greatest inhibitor to attainment in schools is children's self-confidence and level of anxiety. When children feel comfortable and 'at home' in their environment, they are far more likely to succeed. When they are subjected to significant change, it can take many children a long time to adjust to their new situation. During this period of adjustment, their potential for maximum attainment is drastically reduced.

Aims of the case study project

The purpose of the case study project was to take eight different settings in one local authority and work with them to create an approach to transition that minimised the potential for anxiety and maximised the potential for attainment.

The aims of the project were:

- To raise awareness of the principles of effective practice in the EYFS and how this can be developed in Year One.
- To address parents' understanding and awareness of the value of a more play-based curriculum in Year One and to give schools the confidence and tools to promote this.
- To address the concerns of children at transition to Year One.
- To ensure the effective use of assessment at transition to Year One.
- To disseminate good practice from the project schools to all schools across Salford and beyond.

Schools from the local authority were invited for inclusion into the project. The criteria for inclusion were:

- Willingness to allow staff time in Year One and Reception to undertake action research as part of the project (with some supply costs).
- Willingness to use the findings from the research to influence current and future practice.
- Desire to look at policy and practice in Year One in depth and make any appropriate changes.
- Willingness to undertake a whole school approach to successful transition.
- Willingness to share the information with other schools in their locality.
- Willingness to host visits from other practitioners during and after the project.

Getting the project started in the schools

Once the successful schools had been identified, then the project work could begin. Each setting was given a very basic outline of what the focus of the project would be and what they would be expected to produce for the project. We started by looking at the following four action points in each of the project schools:

1. Analyse and document current transition practice to Year One.
2. Look at the environment in Year One – how could it be changed or adapted to ensure:
   - transition is smooth and effective for all children.
   - it is flexible enough so it can be changed and adapted throughout the year.
   - it will provide for continuous provision, both indoors and outdoors, that is stimulating and inviting and will engage and challenge all children and respond to a wide range of learners.
3. What happens at transition in terms of assessment transfer and effective use of the EYFS assessment in Year One?
4. Put plans put in place with short- and long-term actions over the project.

The main indicator for success within the project was going to be based on academic attainment and children's levels of wellbeing and involvement using the Leuven scales. As I have said previously, it is when children feel most comfortable that there is the most potential to engage them in learning.

To allow us to do this, we asked each of the schools to choose six Reception children at the beginning of the project and carry out a wellbeing and involvement assessment on them using the Leuven Scales (see Chapter 1, p.7). This assessment would be carried out again as these children moved into Year One to see if the setting's existing transition arrangements had had any effect on the results.

Once the settings had had a year to work on their transition arrangements, the same process would be carried out again on six Reception children in the Summer term and then again on those children in the Autumn term of Year One to see if the changes that had been made would have any impact on results.

Settings were also asked to keep more detailed learning logs on all six children from each cohort, keeping an example of their reading, writing and mathematics attainment when every Leuven assessment was done. The practitioners themselves were asked to keep a diary that recorded the changes they made to their practice, including both successes and challenges!

Of course, no practitioner research project ever goes as straightforwardly as we would like it to, especially one that spans a considerable length of time. So, during the project there were changes to staffing in the settings and some study children who left. Some settings were able to commit to the project to a greater extent than others.

In the settings that were well supported by their senior management team and where staff made a definite commitment to the project, the impact of the results were more profound.

Out of the eight schools, only two had the same members of staff in the same position at the beginning and the end of the project. This not only had an impact on the running of the project but also on the quality of some of the information that was collected and the understanding of some members of staff around the purpose of the project and their role within it.

Progress during the project

- All settings made some progress, although some made significant progress and others only minimal.
- All settings were up to date with tracking the wellbeing and involvement of the identified children and most had collected both anecdotal and concrete evidence to substantiate their judgements.
- The practitioners' personal reflections were available on request, but again these differed significantly in content and reflection. Some were written and some were verbal.

These differences between the settings are actually beneficial as they provide a rich breadth of experiences and practice which will then make the finished project accessible to practitioners at all stages of their development.

Alongside the distribution of a 'model' transition policy to all of settings (for amendment and agreement), I also:

- Worked with the participants on systems for providing challenge in continuous provision.
- Delivered staff training to help the members of staff to reflect on their practice and improve the possibilities for children.
- Asked all participating schools' headteachers to make a definitive statement about their expectations and aspirations for their Early Years and Key Stage One departments, and reflecting that in the agreed transition policy.
- Gave participants clear expectations about the requirements and time frames for the rest of the project.
- Looked at interim assessments with the participants to see how they showed the impact of transition and academic and personal development.

Process during the project

- A 'baseline' was recorded from each setting based on the wellbeing and involvement scores and academic attainment of the selected group of Reception children in the Summer term 2012.
- A second set of scores were taken from the same children in September 2012 following their transition into Year One.
- Each school documented their current transition practice.
- Most practitioners kept a regular written or verbal log of their perceptions of the project.
- All schools provided end of year scores for their Reception children in 2012 and interim scores for 2013 for comparison.
- All schools discussed what information was passed up from Reception to Year One and if/how it was used 'realistically'.

What the results said

The children who were selected for tracking using the Leuven scales across all eight schools were a broad mix of gender and ability. As some children left during the project and their scores could not be completed, what follows is an average attainment across all children in all schools.

At the start of the project

Wellbeing scores Reception – summer 2012

- average score – four
- highest score – five
- lowest score – two.

Involvement scores Reception – summer 2012

- average score – four
- highest score – five
- lowest score – one.

After transition into Year One

Wellbeing scores Year One – September 2012

- average score – three
- highest score – five
- lowest score – one

Involvement scores Year One – September 2012

- average score – three
- highest score – five
- lowest score – one.

Summary of early findings

- Of the 48 children who were initially selected for tracking through this transition, all 48 were still in place at this point.
- 16 children maintained their scores in both wellbeing and involvement. These children had all scored highly in their Reception assessment.
- 32 children dropped at least one scale point in both wellbeing and involvement following transition.
- The largest drop in score for wellbeing was three points.
- The largest drop in score for involvement was three points.

- In one setting, three of the six children maintained their score in both areas and the other three only dropped one point in either wellbeing or involvement.
- In two settings, all children dropped at least one point in both wellbeing and involvement and some dropped up to three points.

If the two assessments (at the end of Reception and start of Year One) had been carried out by two different practitioners, there would have been a margin for differences in moderation. To counteract this, practitioners were asked to carry out all assessments together. The results at this early stage indicated that the methods used to support children through this period of transition had a significant impact.

During Year One

This cohort of children was assessed again in Spring 2013 and Summer 2013 against the same scales.

Summary of findings during Year One
Wellbeing and involvement:

- 16 children maintained their scores across both of these assessments. Of these 16 children, eight had a maximum score of five in both areas; eight had mid-range scores in both areas and these scores remained the same.
- 16 children increased their scores during the period of assessment.
- Six children made up to two points progress in either wellbeing or involvement, but they did not score the maximum of five in either area.

Academic attainment:

- Unsurprisingly, there was a direct correlation between levels of wellbeing and involvement and academic attainment. For children whose levels of wellbeing and involvement fell on entry to Year One, their academic attainment also dipped.
- Children's attainment also improved in direct correlation to the improvement levels in their wellbeing and involvement.

Evaluating current practice

Once the initial assessments had been carried out, the schools reflected on their current practice for transition. This differed greatly between the settings. Some were at the very beginning of analysing their systems and others were mid-way through a process of re-evaluation.

Environment changes

For some of the settings, creating a more fluid transition meant a significant change to the Year One environment. The project worked on the principle that Year One should prepare their environment to match the environment that exists in Reception at the end of the summer term, not getting Reception 'ready' for Year One.

If the environment was going to look more like Reception, then for some settings their planning also had to change to allow them to plan effectively for the new environment. This presented the first big challenge of the project and helped to shape one of the guiding principles for the resulting transition policy.

Some of the Year One staff reported that they felt underprepared in terms of how to manage the running of the environment and how to use the EYFS document to create effective planning. For some, there had been the purchase of new furniture to bring the environment more in line with Reception. For other settings, this was not the case and the staff struggled to recycle what they had effectively. There was also the issue of storage or disposal of excess furniture and resources.

Some common issues that were raised through the practitioners' personal learning journey entries were:

- They felt they had lost some control over what the children were doing while playing in continuous provision.

- In some settings, the practitioners raised the issue that their headteacher did not support the concept of a Foundation Stage approach to learning in Year One as described. In those cases, the negative impact on children's wellbeing, involvement and attainment was apparent.

- It was also felt that it was hard to track what the children were doing and that some children only played in particular areas of provision therefore appeared not to be getting any breadth in their learning.

In the setting where the transition of the children had been most effective, the Year One practitioner had a very strong knowledge of EYFS practice and liaised with her Reception colleague on a daily basis. When the geography of the setting enhanced and supported a close working relationship between Reception and Year One, it meant that each practitioner was very knowledgeable about the practice of the other and that the children were very comfortable and familiar with all the members of staff in both classes.

Planning and paperwork

Planning effectively for children performing at EYFS level alongside children who are working within the National Curriculum is challenging for any practitioner, especially if your knowledge of one curriculum is stronger than the other.

Staff taking part in the project (particularly in Year One) felt it was essential that they had time to familiarise themselves with the EYFS document and to also have opportunities to see how their colleagues in Reception planned and then executed that planning, working alongside them to give opportunities for questioning and investigation.

As part of the planning process, we looked at the information that was passed up from Reception to Year One and how much of this information was currently used by the Year One staff to inform their initial planning process. The information varied from setting to setting, but the one common issue for most settings was that Reception were producing a great deal of information that wasn't being used in Year One. The reasons for this varied. Some Year One members of staff were unsure about how to interpret the EYFS data and therefore were unable to use it; some felt more secure in carrying out their own assessments at the beginning of the year.

It was felt by all settings that opportunities for professional discussion about the Reception cohort's progress needed to take place with the Year One staff regularly, so that they gained a broad picture of the attainment of the children they would be teaching the following year. This dialogue would also give the Year One members of staff the opportunity to discuss how the opportunities offered to children in Reception could be enhanced to help them with some of the challenges of Year One.

A number of planning formats and routines were discussed with each setting. Regardless of the pro forma that was eventually put in place, the underlying need was one that ensured the planning was based on accurate assessment and that it clearly provided challenge and was evaluated to show attainment.

To ensure that only relevant and useful information was passed up from Reception, a decision about exactly what information would be passed up would be decided on by practitioners from both year groups alongside the school's assessment co-ordinator, rather than on a more ad hoc basis which was the practice of some of the settings.

Building on what children know

One practitioner described children's transition to Year One as 'hitting a brick wall'. In their setting, the changes in EYFS had been huge but this change had not been reflected in Year One where the practice had remained the same. She felt that, as a Year One practitioner, her knowledge of the EYFS curriculum was limited and she found it difficult to interpret the children's attainment based on the profile information that she was provided with. As a result, the children were all completely re-assessed on entry to Year One against National Curriculum expectations. Needless to say there were a number of children whose attainment appeared to go backwards.

Probably the worst time to assess children is on their return to school in September as they have just had the longest break in the school calendar. They are still getting back into the swing of school life as well as getting used to their new teacher and new routines. It is little wonder that they don't perform well in their assessments.

For transition from Reception to Year One to be really effective, Year One practitioners need to have a working knowledge of EYFS and its curriculum and then be able to use the information that they are provided with to ensure their expectations of the children are challenging and based on accurate assessment. The beginning of Year One needs cross-phase planning that looks at each child's stage of development, and not just the year group that they are in.

When settings trialled regular meetings throughout the year between the Reception and Year One staff, they reported that this was highly beneficial as they obtained a very clear picture of the cohort's attainment over time and therefore knew what to expect in terms of attainment in specific areas of the curriculum long before the children moved into their class. It was also found that it was very beneficial for the Reception and Year One staff to meet post-transition. This enabled the Year One staff to talk about how the class was performing, and the Reception staff to compare this to their expectations of each child in both behaviour and attainment.

Continuing professional development (CPD)

Finding time for members of staff to meet in order to fulfil all of the requirements of the transition policy was an issue in most settings. Although all of the suggestions of the policy were thought to be valid and had proved to be effective, it was felt that in order for them to be done thoroughly and to achieve a quality outcome, designated and protected time needed to be given as part of the school's policy for CPD.

Ideally, training on the interpretation of Early Years data should be part of the whole school's agenda for staff training, but at the very least Year One staff need to be given time within the setting's training schedule to become knowledgeable about policy and practice.

Barriers to success

In all settings, the barriers to success that the heads and practitioners identified were remarkably similar. Looking from a whole school perspective, the things that had got in the way of progress were:

- **Staff change** – in schools where there had been little or no change, the project made good progress. In schools where there continued to be changes of leadership and members of staff, the project made limited progress.

- **Staff absence** – schools which had a member of the team who had been absent also made slower progress.

- **Engagement of the head/management team** – in the settings where the head had been proactive in working with the project, good progress had been made.
- **Subject knowledge** – it became clear that settings that had practitioners with a strong subject knowledge and a wealth of experience made good progress, whereas settings where the practitioner knowledge was developing or poor, made slow progress. At times in the settings where practice was poor, the project became more about effective teaching than transition. Also, settings that had a headteacher or management team with a more in-depth knowledge of EYFS made good progress; when their knowledge was limited, so was the progress.

From the practitioner's point of view, some barriers were:

- Time to make the environment really effective.
- A worry that the Year Two teacher would not value the skills that these children have.
- The worry that other staff members would not value/understand exactly what we are trying to achieve.
- The lack of appropriate funding.
- Not having an extra member of staff with responsibility for maintaining the shared area and promoting purposeful use/play within it, which would be a wonderful addition.
- An over-timetabled day and having to find space to teach each of the discreet foundation subjects individually kept the day formal.
- Lack of access to outdoor space.
- A reluctance to scrap previous Year One planning (self-imposed by Year One teachers) and the difficulty of trying to fit in continuous provision.
- How comfortable members of staff felt with a play-based curriculum and their understanding of how to create play-based scenarios for EYFS learning objectives.
- Staff unease at giving adults time to observe and intervene to support learning on all levels of planning across both Reception and Year One – the teacher and TA are always 'teaching' either whole class, or a group of children.
- The majority of Year One children not being able to work on a directed task without adult support (autumn term) – needing lots of training.
- Equipment/furniture not always suitable for the children to self-access equipment.
- Not having a range of resources to keep resources exciting and 'new'.
- Lack of clarity for Year One members of staff about expectations of the project, e.g. who is giving advice/taking decisions.
- Conflicting ideas within senior management as to how Year One should be run, e.g. no prior discussion, guidance or agreement about what changes SLT envisaged for Year

One, and changes sometimes imposed by senior management without consultation with Year One staff.

- Year One lead teacher lacking the experience and confidence to make significant changes in Year One, which potentially could have a negative impact on the results.

The majority of the identified issues are based on pedagogy, practice and understanding. Many of them can be resolved with effective training and development.

Final assessment

In the summer term of 2013, six children from the Reception class of each setting were assessed against the Leuven scales and then in the autumn term they were reassessed on entry to Year One.

- In all settings there was a significant difference in the number of children who maintained their scores during the transition.
- In the settings where there had been the least number of changes in staffing or management during the project, all children maintained their end of Reception scores and in one setting, with very effective and embedded transition arrangements, some children actually increased their score.

What the results said at the end of the project

As before the children who were chosen were tracked using the Leuven scales. Across all eight schools they were a broad mix of gender and ability.

Wellbeing scores Reception summer term 2013

- average score – four
- highest score – five
- lowest score – one.

Involvement scores Reception summer term 2013

- average score – three
- highest score – five
- lowest score – one.

After transition into Year One

Wellbeing scores Year One September 2013

- average score – four
- highest score – five
- lowest score – three.

Involvement scores Year One September 2013

- average score – four
- highest score – five
- lowest score – three.

Summary of findings

- 40 children maintained their scores in both wellbeing and involvement. These children had all scored highly in their Reception assessment.
- No children dropped at least one scale point in both wellbeing and involvement following transition.
- The largest drop in score for wellbeing was one point; the largest drop in score for involvement was one point.
- In one setting, all the children maintained their score in both areas.
- Although the two assessments (at the end of Reception and start of Year One) were carried out by two different practitioners and therefore there is a margin for differences in moderation, the results indicate that the methods used to support children through this period of transition following the implementation of a new policy and practice had a significant impact on both wellbeing and involvement.

The results clearly show that if transition is to be truly effective in maintaining children's interest and enjoyment in school, which will ultimately impact on their potential for attainment, it must be a thought out and valued process.

Across the term of the project, I produced and refined a transition policy incorporating all of the successful strategies that the practitioners had used, and following their feedback. This policy is given here.

Draft transition policy: Reception – KS1

Contents

- Introduction
- Rationale

- Aims
- Equal opportunities and inclusion
- Principles that underpin the policy
- Initial preparations
- Creating an appropriate environment
- Building on what children know and understand
- Partnership with parents
- Continuing Professional Development (CPD)
- Appendices

Introduction

Excellence and Enjoyment discusses broadening and increasing the creativity within Key Stage One to meet the needs of young children. Extending the Foundation Stage curriculum into Key Stage One would address the advice given in this guidance, as well as meeting the needs of younger children as they progress through their learning. In this policy, 'transition' describes the movement that takes place from one year to the next, and in particular from one phase of education to the next within the school. This is different from 'transfer', which describes the movement from one school to the next.

Rationale

At [insert school name] we feel it is important to create a whole school approach of which staff, children, parents, governors and other agencies have a clear understanding. This policy is a formal statement of intent for Reception to KS1 transition. The policy also facilitates how we meet the legal requirements of Education Acts and National Curriculum requirements.

Aims

We want our children to experience a smooth educational and emotional transition from one phase to the next. This will ensure that children make the best all round progress.

Equal opportunities and inclusion

The children and parents are actively involved in the process and their perceptions about transition are explored and valued. There are clear curriculum guidelines for children with learning difficulties during transition. Appropriate assistance will be provided in a variety of ways, including:

- a range of learning styles
- using pupils' ideas and motivations as a starting point for learning
- adjusting the conceptual demand of the task as appropriate for the child.

Principles that underpin the policy

The principles that underpin our transition policy are as follows:

- Approaches to teaching and learning should be harmonised at the point of transition.
- Planning should be based upon assessment information from the previous class/group/setting.
- Styles of teaching and learning should meet the needs of children and not preconceived notions of what is or is not appropriate for the next phase/Key Stage.
- There should be a professional regard for the information from the previous setting/phase.
- Children's emotional welfare, wellbeing and involvement should be assessed before and after transition.
- Children should enjoy the transition process.
- The transition should motivate and challenge children.
- Staff allocation for a period prior to, during and after initial transition should be made to maximise the comfort and welfare of the children.
- Effective transition takes time, and is a process rather than an event.
- Parents and carers need to feel well informed about and comfortable with all transitions in their child's life.
- Children, parents/carers and staff need to be involved on an equal basis.
- Transition is about the setting fitting the child, not the child fitting the setting.
- Transitions are not overlooked or left to chance, but thought about and planned in advance.

Initial preparations

Transitions are not overlooked or left to chance; good transition takes careful thought and thorough planning well in advance. All staff must be aware of the systems that are currently in place and build their review into the school's self-evaluation schedule.

- Year One teachers to spend some designated time in Reception each term, observing children in their familiar environment and observing practice.

- Time is planned for termly meetings between Reception and Year One for teachers to discuss ongoing assessment and profile information.
- Reception and Year One teachers and the assessment co-ordinator should agree together what needs to be handed on at the end of the year.
- Reception children visit Year One a minimum of once per term.
- At least one joint project is planned between Reception and Year One each year.
- Arrangements are made for passing on information to parents about the transition to Year One.
- Reception parents are invited to meet the Year One teacher/support staff (where practicable) and explore the Year One environment.
- Reception teachers are given designated time to observe teaching practice in Year One at least once a term.

Creating an appropriate environment

- The Year One classroom has areas of continuous provision to support and extend children's independence skills.
- All members of staff have received training on how to provide a high-quality learning environment.
- Year One members of staff have visited Reception to see how areas of provision provide support and challenge for children's current learning so that they can ensure future progress in the way they plan and organise their provision.
- The areas of provision in Year One are planned for appropriate learning objectives with more challenge and teacher-focused tasks.
- Children in Year One have access to an outdoor learning environment to support teaching and learning.
- A richly resourced outdoor classroom is used to support teaching and learning in Year One.

Building on what children know and understand

- Areas of provision are planned for Year One, similar to those in Reception, but with appropriate challenge and adult-directed activities.
- Support staff move temporarily or permanently with Reception children to their next class.
- Reception and Year One staff members meet to discuss assessment information.
- Reception teachers highlight those children who are still working at EYFS level or may need a modified curriculum.

- Year One teachers will use cross-phase planning that incorporates both profile scale points and National Curriculum levels.
- Reception and Year One teachers meet in the latter part of the summer term to discuss the possible curriculum and environment for the first half term in Year One.
- Teachers meet after the first few weeks in Year One to discuss individual children after the settling in period.
- Throughout the year, Reception and Year One teachers occasionally teach each other's classes to develop a greater understanding of children's learning and gain knowledge about the curriculum.

Partnership with parents

At [school name] we encourage parents to be involved by:

- Inviting parents into school three times a year to discuss the progress of their child.
- Inviting parents into school in the summer term to discuss the annual report.
- Inviting parents to curriculum evenings.
- Sending parents half-termly information booklets/newsletters to inform parents of curriculum coverage.
- Encouraging parents to come in and help in the classroom. [Add individual practice.]
- Parents are informed in the summer term about the class that their child will be in.
- Parents are given clear information about what to expect in Year One.
- Parents are given the opportunity to meet the Year One staff before September.
- Parents are invited to experience the Year One environment, classroom layout and resources before September.
- Reception parents are invited to help out in Year One.
- Parents are invited to an information evening outlining what the National Curriculum is, and how best to support their child's learning in Year One.
- Brief end of the day 'open door' sessions are offered to parents in the first few weeks of Year One to address any issues regarding their child settling into Year One.

Continuing Professional Development (CPD)

- Reception and Year One teachers know what the EYFS profile contains and how to interpret the scale points.
- Reception and Year One teachers know how the EYFS curriculum links to the National Curriculum.

- Reception and Year One teachers are confident in making assessments through the observation of children.
- Reception and Year One teachers plan collaboratively checking that continuity and progressions are evident from Reception to Year One.
- Professional development opportunities in relation to transition are evident in the school improvement plan.

Appendices

Could include:

- a resources list
- a transition action plan
- examples of profile point moderation
- references to appropriate relevant information.

9 A transition diary

As I have already discussed throughout this book, transition is not an event – it doesn't just happen in the last couple of weeks of term. For a transition to be truly effective it has to be planned and delivered over a period of time enabling children (and adults) to become familiar with how the process will work.

This transition diary is meant to be a starting point to help you to plan your transition from Reception to Year One. You can, of course, amend it and add to it all of the unique and individual things that you do to make sure you get the most effective transition possible.

A year of transition – a guide for Year One teachers

September

- After the discussed transition procedures, settle in your new children. Establish rules and routines for the new way of working. Keep tissues handy for anyone who cries (children and staff!). Make a concerted effort not to get frustrated when the children ask a) if they can go and play now, b) when outside will be open, c) if it is mummy time yet.
- If possible, arrange to take some transition staff from Reception (permanently or temporarily) into Year One. This could be as simple as just having a familiar face from Reception to welcome the children to teaching or support staff moving into Year One for the academic year.
- Have a period of 'drop in' at the end of the day for Year One parents to help them to adjust to the transition.
- After about three weeks, carry out Leuven Scale assessment on the six children that were identified as a representative group in Reception.
- Send home information to parents about the transition and how it is working and curriculum coverage.
- Ensure at least one staff meeting is given over to EYFS training for Year One staff this term.

October

- Make your first visit to Reception to 'experience' next year's cohort – it is a really important part of the transition process that Year One teachers can get to see first hand the level that children enter Reception.

- Share your point of entry assessment of your Year One children with the Reception staff – in Year One you will have had your data from Reception to use as a starting point. Although accurate at the time, children have had a long period away from school and it may take them a while to get back up to speed. By October half term, Year One staff can give feedback to Reception staff about how their children are settling emotionally and academically.

- Reception staff to share their baseline assessment of their new cohort with Year One staff so that everyone is aware of the priorities for progress and you can share advice.

- Reception staff to share their first GSA with Year One and talk them through their environment plan.

- Reception staff should be able to talk to Year One about their foci for direct teaching and how they have planned their continuous provision in relation to common play behaviours.

- Arrange a story swap (or similar activity) so you go to Reception to work with them or they come to you.

November

- Arrange your first official adult share or swap. This will be your first of three (minimum) adult shares or swaps.

- If you can arrange to be released from your class for the day then go and spend it working alongside your Reception colleague. Have a meeting to talk about the planning process first, e.g. discuss how the continuous provision has been enhanced, etc. Make sure you have time to discuss and feedback at the end of the day (before you have a lie down in a darkened room!).

- It is important that Year One adults get the chance to visit Reception for this process, but equally as important that Reception staff get to do the same in Year One. Not only is it important for Reception staff to be aware of the demands of the Year One curriculum, it is also brilliant for them to see what their old class is up to! This initiative is not just about teachers, support staff will benefit equally as well from this type of share or swap.

- Arrange a story swap (or similar activity) so you go to Reception to work with them or they come to you.

- Reception children visit and spend some time in the Year One space.

- Send home information to parents about the transition, how it is working and curriculum coverage.

December

- Hold on tight, Christmas is coming!
- Reception staff are probably carrying out their second summative assessment – make sure that you make the time to share the results of that assessment, look at how it translates into GSA and how that in turn affects the continuous provision as well as the direct teaching.
- Try and fit in another couple of brief visits to Reception to get a 'feel' for how it works and get to know your children. Come and sit in their snack area during your playtime or come and be their 'secret' storyteller at the end of the day.
- Arrange a story swap (or similar activity) so you go to Reception to work with them or they come to you.

January

- Carry out Leuven scale assessment on the six identified children to assess current wellbeing and involvement.
- Arrange a story swap (or similar activity) so you go to Reception to work with them or they come to you.
- Ensure at least one staff meeting is given over to EYFS training for Year One staff this term.
- Send home information to parents about the transition, how it is working and curriculum coverage.

February

- Reception may be carrying out another summative assessment. If so, make sure that you make the time to share the results of that assessment, look at how it translates into GSA and how that in turn affects the continuous provision as well as the direct teaching.
- Arrange a joint moderation meeting between Reception and Year One to share and validate judgements.
- Think about arranging a joint 'event' with Reception and Year One. Anything from a special class assembly to a trip or experience.
- Arrange a story swap (or similar activity) so you go to Reception to work with them or they come to you.

March

- Plan in your second share or swap to observe how practice and progress have moved on.

- Arrange a story swap (or similar activity) so you go to Reception to work with them or they come to you.

- Reception children visit and spend time in the Year One space.

- Send home information to parents about the transition, how it is working and curriculum coverage.

April

- Reception staff are probably carrying out another summative assessment. Make sure that you make the time to share the results of that assessment, look at how it translates into GSA and how that in turn affects the continuous provision as well as the direct teaching.

- Arrange a story swap (or similar activity) so you go to Reception to work with them or they come to you.

- Send home information to parents about the transition, how it is working and curriculum coverage.

- Ensure at least one staff meeting is given over to EYFS training for Year One staff this term.

May

- Arrange a joint moderation meeting between Reception and Year One to share and validate judgements.

- Arrange a story swap (or similar activity) so you go to Reception to work with them or they come to you.

- Send home information to parents about the transition, how it is working and curriculum coverage.

June

- Plan in your final share or swap to observe how practice and progress have moved on.

- Arrange a story swap (or similar activity) so you go to Reception to work with them or they come to you.

- Reception children visit and spend time in the Year One space.

- Invite parents to a curriculum evening about transition and expectations in Year One.

July

- Invite the parents of next year's intake to come in and have a look at the Year One environment. Set it up as it will be on point of entry to Year One. Have lots of examples of Year One children's work to share to celebrate progress and attainment.

- Take copies of Reception's final GSA as well as their common play behaviours for continuous provision. This is your ready-made map for your areas of provision and resources for September.

- Strip your classroom and prepare your transition display. Invite the Reception children to bring you the piece of work they are most proud of to be displayed on your wall.

- Choose six children from Reception to take part in a Leuven Scale assessment now and again in September once they have entered Year One.

Conclusion

Well done for making it to the end of the book – or just flicking to the last bit in the hope that I will summarise it in the conclusion (good thinking)! I have written a lot in the preceding chapters about what makes an effective transition into Year One. Some of it I am hoping will be familiar to some of you, but for some I suspect it will be a million miles away from what your school already do. Many of you may still be thinking that you get the idea but are wary of starting down a play-based route because if it all goes wrong then when will the children actually learn anything? For some of you I imagine that you are still trying to get to grips with the use of the term 'play' in Year One.

Fundamentally, what we are talking about is best outcomes for children. There, that has summed up a whole book in one sentence! The trickier bit is getting to the root of how we achieve those best outcomes. By that I don't just mean best results or best test scores, I mean best outcomes for *all* children. For the more mature, more accomplished children who are easily meeting their Early Learning Goals by the end of the Reception year *and* the less mature, less academically accomplished children who will still be striving to meet theirs well into Year One and for some, even beyond that.

Traditional Year One teaching methods have been with us for a *long* time. Even though a lot of the technology has changed and our children are now looking at a whiteboard rather than a blackboard, the systems have remained static and the process not dissimilar in essence to that of the Victorian era.

One area of education that has taken a huge shift over the last decade or so, is the teaching of the children at the very beginning of the learning process in what we now know of as the Early Years Foundation Stage. A huge amount of research has been done into the most effective way of engaging children's developing brains in the learning process. Some of that has been ground breaking brain research and a lot has just been common sense. The conclusion? Children learn best through self-motivated play with the support and regular input of adults in a well-structured environment. So, why should that be any different for children in Year One (or the rest of the school for that matter)? When children reach Year One they are only five or six weeks older than they were when they left Reception so why the dramatic change in recommendations, curriculum, environment and routine?

During their summer absence from school we know that the children are not likely to have improved their level of knowledge. If anything, because they are not practising their skills on a daily basis, being reminded of what they need to know and encouraged to apply what they have learned, they are likely to forget a portion of what they know. With the lack of school routine, the learning bit of their brain gets a bit 'dusty' over the summer and some bits of last-minute learning and GLD 'cramming' get lost or leak out when they are asleep.

When they return to you in Year One, they are not even starting from a level playing field. They need time to spring clean the dusty bits of their brains, to remember, recall and revisit and that takes time – for some children, a lot more time than others.

Where would be the best place for this reminding and revisiting of knowledge? In the space where they first acquired it and with the people who imparted it to them. Why? Because the space is familiar. They know how it works – the rules, routines, expectations and resources. The people are familiar they have established a relationship of support and trust; the space and the people make them feel secure.

It is when children feel that sense of security that their brain needs to concentrate less on their survival instinct and can focus on the other bits like learning. It stands to reason then that if we want the best emotionally and academically from our children on entry to Year One, we would try and make as much of their environment as similar as we possibly could to the one that they left in Reception. If we don't, far from promoting an environment for high-level attainment, we run the risk of setting their progress even further back. This scenario doesn't just apply to the children who did not make their GLD by the end of Reception. All of my transition project research has shown that when we use the Leuven Scales to assess children's levels of wellbeing and involvement, that a significant number of the children who showed a higher level of academic attainment at the end of Reception reduced their Leuven Scores on entry to Year One.

How often have you been frustrated as a Year One practitioner that the children you have got sitting in front of you on your September carpet are not the same ones you had passed up to you in the end of EYFS assessment data? It is not that the assessment is necessarily incorrect – just that the children are being, well, children who have just had a prolonged period away from learning and are now in a relatively alien space, with a lovely but relatively alien teacher following a completely alien routine. We wouldn't be very happy either.

Many of the principles of effective transition to Year One are based on the concept of 'similarity' or 'sameness'. Some settings have found great success by taking the Reception teacher and the children into Year One together, maintaining that level of familiarity, trust and expectation. For schools who can't or choose not to do that, then we have to make the transition as smooth as it can possibly be.

If the people are not going to be the same ones that we saw every day in Reception, then we have to make them as familiar as possible. This you can achieve through regular visits, joint projects, story swaps, teaching swaps and just being a regular visitor to EYFS,

If we are not going to be taught in the same learning space, then we need to make the new one as similar to the old one as possible. If the children had a quality learning space in Reception, then they are not going to have any learning 'slippage' if Year One looks the same. In truth, their levels of wellbeing and security are likely to rise at a much faster pace making them more receptive to learning and able to achieve progress far quicker, which has a more drastic impact on standards of attainment in the future.

If you have never taught in Early Years before and haven't received any specific Early Years training then you will find running an Early Years classroom and timetable very different from Year One. This is another reason why the transition process is a long-term project and not something that just happened in the last couple of weeks of term. If you know you are going to run your Year One classroom as close to a Foundation Stage approach as you can get it, then you need to have a good idea what that is going to look like.

You also want to make sure you are providing quality play experiences for children linked to skills that they have already acquired and using resources that have the potential to take their learning forward, not invite them back to using low-level skills that are well rehearsed and therefore result in learning stagnation as opposed to progress.

If your Early Years team are already using ongoing and summative assessment to plan their environment, then a great deal of your job will have been done for you with regard to the initial stages of your planning and preparation. You will be able to use their GSA (or similar) to plot your areas for development and those you need to further challenge children's learning. This is turn will help you to plan areas of provision for the children to work in. It is worth thinking about a transfer of resources from the end of Reception to the beginning of Year One, as they will suit the needs of your children, but will be too advanced for the needs of the incoming Reception children.

The final piece in your puzzle is the combination and execution of adult delivery and the child-initiated learning. Again, I have written a great deal about what it is possible to do in your Year One classroom and what will get you the best results. But, everyone is at a different stage in their experience of play-based transition and their understanding of the Early Years Foundation Stage. So, it is important that you try and work a model that suits your (and your team's) current level of understanding and comfort. It is no use throwing caution to the wind and saying that you are going to have long sessions of continuous provision and that adults will only deliver using objective-led planning if you are not really secure with what it is and how it works.

Put together a transition plan that you think will work for you, while at the same time making provision to skill yourself up in all of the areas that you don't yet understand. Even if you can see the sense in the theory, it is nothing without the understanding and a bit of practice. Also, you probably haven't just got you to consider, there will be any other members of staff who work with you to explain it all to. Not to mention any parents who ask why they are still 'playing' in Year One. So, make a realistic plan and stick to it.

Some of the most invaluable sessions that you will spend in Reception will be the ones when you are shadowing, observing practice and doing some teacher swaps. They are the ones that get most easily forgotten and swallowed up in a sea of 'jobs', but they are really useful and informative, so make sure that you plan them in.

Effective play-based transition can have a really powerful effect on all children, capitalising on what they know and how they learned it, enabling them to be the best that they can be in Year One.

Happy children make successful learners (and happy teachers)!

Bibliography and further reading

Bryce-Clegg, A. (2013), *Continuous Provision in the Early Years: How to Plan Provision to Make a Positive Impact on Children's Learning*. Featherstone Education.

Bryce-Clegg, A. (2015), *Continuous Provision: The Skills*. Featherstone Education.

Bryce-Clegg, A. (2013), *Getting Ready to Write: Improving Provision and Outcomes for the Children in Your Setting*. Featherstone Education.

DfE (2005), 'Excellence and Enjoyment: *Social and Emotional Aspects of Learning Guidance*'. Crown copyright. (http://www.education.gov.uk/publications/eOrderingDownload/DFES0110200MIG2122.pdf)

DfE (2013), 'Early Years Outcomes: A Non-statutory Guide for Practitioners and Inspectors to Help Inform understanding of Child Development Through the Early Years'. Crown copyright. (www.foundationyears.org.uk/wp-content/uploads/2012/03/Early_Years_Outcomes.pdf)

DfE (2015), 'Early years foundation stage profile results in England, 2015'. DfE and National Statistics. Crown copyright.

Dowling, M. (2013), *Young Children's Thinking*. SAGE Publications.

Early Education (2012), 'Development Matters in the Early Years Foundation Stage (EYFS)'. Crown copyright. (www.early-education.org.uk/development-matters-early-years-foundation-stage-eyfs-download)

Rutherford, Nichola (2016), 'Should the school starting age be raised to seven?'. BBC Scotland. (www.bbc.co.uk/news/uk-scotland-35401265)

World Health Organisation (2015), 'Gender fact sheet no. 403'. (www.who.int/gender-equity-rights/understanding/gender-definition/en/)

Index